APAL
EMPOWERMENT SCHEME IN THE STATE OF OSUN, NIGERIA

Wumi Raji

APALARA: YOUTH EMPOWERMENT SCHEME IN THE STATE OF OSUN, NIGERIA

Wumi Raji

Research Assistants
Adetokunbo Shittu
Folasade Adewale – Lawal

GALDA VERLAG 2022

Bibliografische Information der Deutschen Nationalbibliothek
Die Deutsche Nationalbibliothek verzeichnet diese Publikation in der Deutschen Nationalbibliografie; detaillierte bibliografische Daten sind im Internet über https://dnb.de abrufbar.

Galda Verlag, Franz-Schubert-Str. 61, 16548 Glienicke, Germany

ISBN 978-3-96203-209-8 (Print)
ISBN 978-3-96203-210-4 (E-Book)

PREFACE

From the first scrap I reacted to with a little caution, Dr Raji has produced a work that does great credit to the idea of fighting youth frustration, opening the door to a healthier work ethic and demonstrating the capacity of good political leadership; for not only stopping the rot in a third world economy and society, but giving a moral boost to the governed, through a peculiar and new form of democracy, as argued in the Irogbo Declaration.

As philosophy, pedagogy, transformation agency and movement, OYES has more than proved itself and Dr Raji has driven this home well in his precise and accurate presentation of records, experiences and hopes of our youth. Dr Raji should also be credited with providing a balanced accreditation of the minds and hands that conceived the idea, constructed the infrastructure and implemented a programme worthy of emulation .

In the beginning, there was a 'Prophet' unarmed. He was driven by a small band of faithful 'apostles' who persisted in their faith and conviction that Osun was not only conquerable from those we then described as barbarians, but that it is also a perfect platform for social engineering and jump-off point for the peace and progress promised at Kiriji, and which must be taken to all parts of the Nigerian State, Africa and, as well, the Diaspora.

OYES as Dr Raji has presented it in this very readable book, is proof of the possible, and Osun youth has tasted of it. I would have loved to see a photograph of the rush for the application forms and declarations by young men and women to whom the idea and programme lit a torch in some cases after five to ten years of successful tertiary education and literally...nothing to do, as their self esteem withered and faith in Western education was put on trial.

The book is also a much needed account of the work and dedication of FORA, the charisma of the Oranmiyan of our time, and all who made, and continue to make OYES, a dream turned reality; and, of course, PFG a realizable dream.

Ambassador T.A.O. Otunla.

ACKNOWLEDGEMENTS

I am grateful to Ogbeni Rauf Aregbesola, governor of the State of Osun, 2010 to 2018, for giving me an express go-ahead when I first approached him with the idea of doing a book on the Osun Youth Empowerment Scheme (OYES). I thank Kola Omotunde-Young, PFG member, who actually drew my attention to OYES and what it represented, and facilitated my contact with Aregbesola when eventually I made up my mind to do the book. The assistance which Mr. Omotunde-Young provided me while working on the project is simply immeasurable, and I hereby seize this opportunity to put my profound appreciation for it on record. My gratitude to Col. Eniibukun Oyewole (rtd), the Commandante of OYES for welcoming me when I went knocking at the door of his office. Beside granting me one of the very first interviews I conducted on the project, he also linked me up with a lot of people who were strategic to the project, made a wealth of materials – including documents and photographs - available to me, and was ever ready to provide me with information and clarifications on all issues I approached him on. Thanks to Mr. Femi Ifaturoti, Head of OYES' Implementation Committee for the strong support; and Mr. Gbenga Odulaja and Femi Oyedele who also served on the same committee. My appreciation to all the direct and indirect beneficiaries of the scheme whom I interacted with in the course of my research. They are too numerous to mention but I have included the interviews I conducted with a number of them as part of the appendices to the book. Thanks to Tokunbo Shittu and Folasade Adewale-Lawal, my two research assistants on the project. I want to as well register my profound appreciation for Ambassador Otunla, a solid intellectual, profound man of the left; and ideological and spiritual backbone of PFG and the administration of Aregbesola. Ambassador Otunla read every single word of this book as I drafted it, made valuable suggestions as I went along, and read the entire manuscript again when it became ready. I cherish the interview he granted me, the suggestions he proffered as I worked on the book and the principles he stood for. I salute him.

Finally, I thank the Alexander von Humboldt Foundation, Bonn, Germany for the three-month renewed research stay granted me in 2018. It was during the period of the visit, utilized at the Technical University of Dresden, Germany, that I finalized work on the manuscript of this book.

TABLE OF CONTENTS

CHAPTER ONE

OSUN YOUTH EMPOWERMENT SCHEME: THE BIRTH OF AN IDEA

The idea that led to the birth of Osun Youth Empowerment Scheme had a long period of gestation, pre-dating the assumption of office of Rauf Aregbesola as governor of the state on November 27, 2010 by a few years. Indeed, Aregbesola, the man, had, for several years been associated with a small group of people who could guardedly be described as idealists. Guardedly because they were no hard core ideologues – at least not many of them - but idealists all the same because they held strong views on what governance ought to be about. Their obsession, specifically, is with the Africans, whom they felt had been consigned to the bottom of the ladder of progress. The world has continued to move on at a fast pace, modernising rapidly but Africans, wherever you find them, and as this group contends, are concerned only with the question of survival, even at a lower than basic level. Given this reality, and as members of this group further insists, governance in any part of the continent, and at whatever level, must not just be about winning elections but, rather, about catering for the interests of the disadvantaged majority, the truly wretched of the earth.

The group did not leave the definition of those who constitute the subject of its obsession hanging. It identified two demographic groups whose interests it thought should represent the concern of any government; with the first being the peasants who depend on subsistence agriculture, and the second, the youth.

The group itself underwent a process of complex transformations and metamorphosis but its beginning went to the time when Aregbesola was still serving as a commissioner in Lagos State. Probably the first to come of these complex processes was the formation of a small association known as FORA which, in full, means Friends of Rauf Aregbesola. As its names suggests, FORA comprised a group of friends of Aregbesola who were organizing activities that touched on the lives of young people.

As Femi Ifaturoti who was a prominent member of the group revealed to this writer in an interview, members of FORA were all, without exception, volunteers. The formation of the group was entirely their initiative. The activities they engaged in were completely their decisions. Since Aregbesola was still, at the time, a cabinet member in Lagos, it was the aim of FORA to begin some kind of sensitization work for what at the time still remained an idea while making sure that their man was not distracted from his primary assignment as Commissioner for Works and Infrastructure. It was part of the strategy of the group to ensure that people were engaged at several levels. Membership of the group comprised a number of his associates in the government of Lagos state, long time friends and compatriots who were just concerned about what was happening in Osun, and who felt convinced about the need for change. As it happened, many of them are not indigenes of Osun, but rather people who shared a similar vision, were concerned about what was happening in the then sleepy state, and jointly believed in the need to alter the course of events, and their collective ability to bring about this desired transformation.

Because Aregbesola was a commissioner then, and there were things he needed to be doing on a regular basis that, as an honest person, his income as a commissioner would not be sufficient for - this, even when he held the all important portfolio of commissioner for works – members of FORA decided to sponsor their own activities independently of the man. In any case, those who know Aregbesola have always readily testified to his belief that public office never represented an avenue for self enrichment but, rather, an opportunity to render service. Given this, it was clear to those who came together to form FORA that they would have to devise independent means of generating funds for their own activities. So, to solve the problem, what they did, in the main, was to levy themselves. In addition, they also sought, and received, donations from well-placed individuals who, although believed in the group's vision and mission, could not, due to one reason or the other, come out openly to declare their support for it.

So what was the ultimate mission of FORA? It was, to put it plainly, to unseat the man laying claim to the governorship position in the state of Osun come 2007, and replace him with an individual who shared their own vision of what governance ought to be about; and, as it happened, the person that had been identified for the purpose was Rauf Adesoji Aregbesola!

It was no doubt an audacious aim, especially when it is considered that the man they were trying to displace was a former military man. So, using the platform of FORA, what the group did was to draw public awareness to the parlous condition of things in the state of Osun, and invite attention to the person who they were proposing as the alternative. They used the media to great advantage in this regard. They appeared regularly on the few television stations that were at the time friendly to them. These included Channels, Galaxy, Sunrise, AIT and so on. Public television stations like NTA and Osun State Broadcasting Corporation (OSBC) were absolutely no go areas at the time; but they managed to place periodic adverts in the newspapers when situations arose that required such urgent actions. They did this especially on days that were considered important in the life of the person they had now placed at the centre of their scheme, his birthdays most notably.

Femi Ifaturoti in the interview that had earlier been referred to underscored the tremendous support that FORA received in Lagos and, as well, the wide reach of the activities they carried out in the various media. Beside him, other prominent members of the movement included Ambassador A. O. Otunla, Charles Akinola, Jide Omoworare, Ade Awobiyi and Tomi Adejuyigbe. At this point, what ought to be underscored is that, much against the unfortunate trend in Nigerian politics, what brought these people together had nothing to do with such sentimental factors as ethnicity or religion but, rather, issues bordering on ideology and/or programme.

Yet, the group had a big limitation, and this lay in the fact that it was not based on the ground, either in the sense of being physically rooted in Osogbo, the state capital, or in any other major town in Osun State; or in the nature of activities it, in the main, carried out. Herein laid then the major appeal of a second group, this time known as Oranyan.

This time around, Rauf Aregbesola had something to do with the initiative that led to the formation of Oranyan. The choice of a name for the group was influenced by the story of the legendary king of the Yoruba of the same name. As the legend has it, Oranyan was a prince of Ile Ife and actually, the last son of Oduduwa, the acclaimed primogenitor of Yoruba race. He was said to have spent much time in exile, during which period he founded Oyo, ruling it as its first Alaafin before moving on to discover Benin, the city which today represents the capital of Edo State. As it happened in this case, it was Eweka I, one of Oranyan's children who would rule Benin as its first Oba. But after sojourning in strange lands for a long time, Oranyan returned to Ife to claim his father's throne.

Applied to the current context, Aregbesola, logically, was the new Oranyan. Like the Oranyan of old, he had traversed strange places and achieved great feats. Particularly, he had become highly influential in Lagos

State, in actual fact, the most respected politician in Alimosho, the largest Local Government area in the state. What was more; he was the chairman of Asiwaju Bola Tinubu's campaign organization in the 1999 governorship election in Lagos state. Indeed, as at the time the group known as Oranyan was being inaugurated, he was the Commissioner for Works and Infrastructure in the same Lagos state. Now, just as Oranyan of old did, Aregbesola was now set to return to his home state to take over the number one position. And, as it was said of Oranyan, he was determined to provide exemplary leadership.

As was the case with FORA, the group now known as Oranyan had the aim of raising the consciousness of the people. It however started off by working like an innocuous organization, operating quietly and moving stealthily. It began by holding regular meetings in the office of the Lagos State Commissioner for Works and Infrastructure where it worked out a careful agenda for itself, revising it again and again. Having satisfied themselves that they now had a good plan of activities, members of Oranyan now set a date for the formal launching of the organization in Osogbo. It fixed August 30, 2005 for the purpose.

The ruling government in Osun at the time did everything to prevent the formal inauguration of the organisation. As the date set for the event drew near, and under the excuse of preventing threat to security and breach of the peace in the state, government announced a number of measures the aim of which was to screen people entering the state. Most notable among these were the road blocks mounted at all the gateways leading to the state capital. In spite of this, and to the amazement of Prince Olagunsoye Oyinlola, the then state governor, the inauguration took place successfully. It was attended by a mammoth crowd, the like, again as Femi Ifaturoti put it in the same interview, that had never before been witnessed in the state, and which was not to be witnessed again, not even in the subsequent campaigns that heralded the election.

From then on, there was no stopping Oranyan. Now openly defiant of the administration, it organized one programme after another, engaging youth, women, farmers, peasants and artisans and, indeed, all disaffected groups. The activities were to dovetail into formal campaigns when, eventually, Aregbesola became the governorship candidate of Action Congress (AC) in the 2007 general elections.

Beside Oranyan, the aim of which was manifestly political, one other important programme which associates of Aregbesola put up during this period was the one known as Spring Board Youth Development Programme (SYDP).

Directly, SYDP came up in response to the consistently poor performances of candidates from the state in the West African School Certificate Examinations (WASCE) and the higher institutions entrance examinations organized by the Joint Admissions Examination Board (JAMB). Operating from the conviction that nobody was created without some learning capacity – once allowances were made, that is, for the various categories of mentally challenged individuals – those behind SYDP tried to proffer scientific explanations for the embarrassing results which pupils from the state continued to post in the two examinations on a yearly basis. Eventually, and again as Femi Ifaturoti posited, the conclusion which SYDP drew was to the effect that such below average feats in examinations could only be due to a combination of factors like family background, poor condition of learning and incompetence, and/or lack of motivation on the part of the teaching staff. Surely, a hungry child was not likely to respond to lessons the way his/her well fed counterpart did, and the one being taught in dilapidated classroom with absolutely no facilities would not be able to assimilate as much as – if at all – the one who had the most recent audio visual equipment before him/her even as lessons were being delivered. Thus convinced, these idealistic men and women decided to intervene. They decided to launch remedial teaching programme for students preparing for either or both examinations - and at no cost to those who were to enlist on it! Different people were assigned to different senatorial zones. Centres were identified. Programme duration was set at eleven weeks and fixed for holiday periods. Teachers were recruited and remunerations decided. In this regard, emphasis was placed more on WAEC examiners. This was based on the belief that those who had prior experience grading WAEC scripts would be able to guide students properly on how to go about answering questions. Having sorted out all this, the programme was advertised in the press. Flyers were also taken to the market and distributed. Applications were not long in coming. Actually it was a deluge. But since resources were limited, selection had to be done. It was, to say the least, a difficult process. In the end the coaching started. For those who benefited from the programme over the three-year period, and again according to Ifaturoti, the success story particularly in the WASC examinations was never below 97%.

Out of these different groups emerged eventually the core which would come to be known as PFG. The acronym stands for *People Friendly Government* and served both as banner for the group and the expression of the vision that brought the members together in the first place. In short, the message these people tried to pass across through the name is that Aregbesola's mandate, when eventually he assumed the governorship mantle in the state of Osun, would be to establish a people friendly government.

PFG had only five members. They were Ambassador T. A.O. Otunla, Barrister Femi Ifaturoti, Mr. Kola Omotunde -Young, Dr. Charles Akinola and Ogbeni Aregbesola himself. It was a kind of motley group. Otunla is a diplomat, as can be seen from his title while the next three are technocrats. Aregbesola is the only career politician among them. Again, not all of them were from the State of Osun. What united them however lay in the simple fact of their being intelligent and energetic individuals. All five of them though were mutual friends and compatriots, committed without exception to the goal of winning the governorship seat in Osun for the group, and with Aregbesola in the driver's position. Regardless of where they came from, each one of them was well acquainted with the terrain of the state that used to be known as at then as the State of the Living Spring.

PFG was inaugurated as part of Irogbo declaration. Irogbo, by the way, is the ancestral village of Rauf Aregbesola. It is a tiny community located close to Ilesa. Aregbesola had donated a Health Centre to the community while still serving as commissioner in Lagos State and it was at the commissioning of this Health Centre that PFG was unveiled. A lot of people were invited to the ceremony and the original plan was to spend three days in the village deliberating on, and fashioning out, a direction for the future government of Aregbesola in Osun state. As it happened, the plan to spend time in the village had to be abandoned as a consequence of the uncongenial security reports that were received. Aregbesola himself could not attend the event and the declaration was read on his behalf by Timothy Owoeye, who, at the time, was the Minority Leader in the Osun State House of Assembly. Currently, He would later transform to the position of Majority Leader in the state's House of Assembly, when ACN eventually took majority of the membership of the Assembly.

Irogbo Declaration gave expression to the kind of goals that the group planned to pursue after taking over the reins of administration in the state of Osun, and with Aregbesola as the governor. The opening statement is more or less a para -phrase of the first paragraph of the Communist Manifesto authored jointly by Karl Marx and Friedrich Engels, asserting that governance throughout the ages has been propelled by either of two kinds of visions: one protecting class interests and the other defending the general interests of the governed. Pledging to be guided by the second vision if its dream to take over the state was actualized, the group promised in the declaration to establish a People Friendly Government as soon as it had been sworn in. In defining what people Friendly Government meant, the declaration makes it clear that it has been guided by the Yoruba ethical philosophy of Omoluabi. Going back in history, the declaration states and I quote:

> In the South-western corner of what is today's Nigeria 'the Yoruba had created IFA as a knowledge system for managing the human condition for the benefit and advantage of the individual and the community. Their social and political organizations were advanced; their textile technology included the production of silk at a time Europe imported silk from the Orient. They created a food technology and agricultural system and culture that sustained a good quality of life to millions of their people. They paraded works of art, of unique creativity including the lost wax process etc. They established an intricate socio-political system and a constitutional monarchy which antedates the failed European experience where over ninety percent of the monarchies are extinct.

In its administration of the state then, PFG promised to be guided by the inspiration provided by the indigenous Yoruba political system which it asserted was itself guided by a humanist philosophy, and which respected the dignity of all citizens and emphasized people's right to "good life." It promised to make a clean break with the government it was trying to unseat, a government which, as it contended, simply subjected the people to "hell on earth." And, finally, it declares:

> It is the acknowledgment of these birthrights and the moral duty to organize, deliver and defend them that is the philosophical imperative of PEOPLE FRIENDLY GOVERNANCE- The operational principles are the firing of the urge, the rational organization of societies, peoples and communities to ensure that political life and space make possible the following:
>
> (a) Sustainable food security
>
> (b) Full employment for youth and all persons of working age
>
> (c) Creative Education and the provision of modern skills capacity
>
> (d) Modern health care delivery system
>
> (e) Prosperity in our time
>
> (f) Peace and general progress for all.

The retreat that was abandoned in Irogbo was later to take place in Lagos. In addition to PFG members, participants at the retreat included a selection of other members of FORA and several other colleagues of Aregbesola in the Lagos State Government. Here it was resolved openly that the new government must be a "People Friendly Government", one "that (would) exist solely for the welfare of the people."

Following the retreat, it was the PFG team of Ambassador Otunla, Kola Omotunde -Young, Femi Ifaturoti, Charles Akinola and Ogbeni himself that would sit down to produce the "green book", a document which would now be titled, "My Pact with the People of Osun State" and which would articulate the summary of his plans of action, – a manifesto, to state it directly – when he assumed duty as the governor of Osun State. It was a bilingual document, produced precisely in English and Yoruba, and published back-to-back, with the English version going by the title "My Pact with the People of Osun State" and the Yoruba version "Majemu mi Pelu awon Eniyan Ipinle Osun."

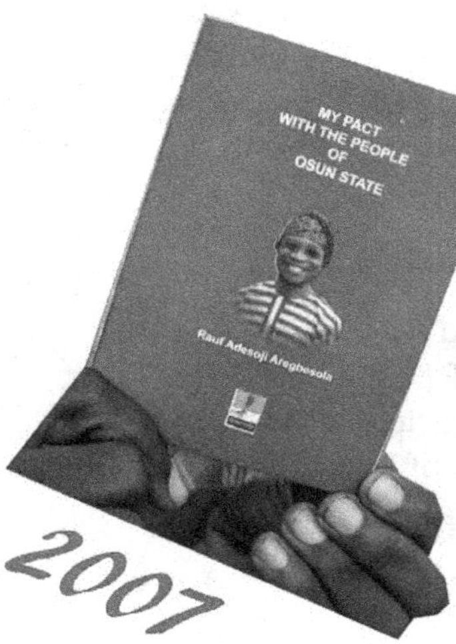

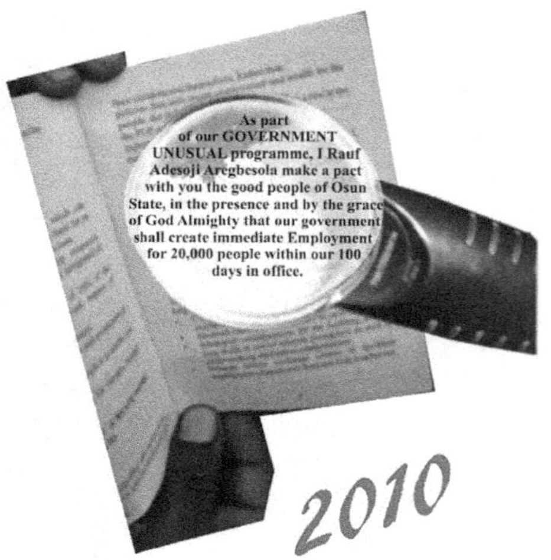

"My Pact" commenced with a preamble which traced a relevant aspect of Yoruba history. It went back to 1886 when, following a series of internecine wars among the Yoruba which went on for close to two decades, the people's leaders came together to sign a treaty which committed them henceforth to the pursuit of peace, progress and development of Yoruba land. As the document asserts, the people would, for the next eighty years or so devote themselves solely to the pursuit of the terms of the treaty, and the result was the unprecedented development witnessed in different parts of what would later become the

Western Region of Nigeria. Precisely, and as the document states, this pursuit of progress was disrupted with the sacking of the Western House of Assembly in 1962 and consequent destruction of the Federal system of government which had operated in the country. Since then, and as "we approach the 2007 general elections, peace, progress and prosperity can no longer be taken for granted amongst us" (My Pact, 2). On the contrary, what obtained, and as the document states further, were "political disenfranchisement, economic stagnation and socio-psychological insecurity." It was against this background, and as the preamble concludes, that PFG and other patriotic individuals took a decision to put Aregbesola forward for the governorship election in the state of Osun.

The Six Point Integral Action Plan

"My Pact with the People of Osun" makes it clear through the manifesto that the kind of government that would be inaugurated after Aregbesola had won the 2007 Osun State governorship election would be known as "Government Unusual", one that would be "totally committed to unlocking the latent potentials in our people" and the type that had not been witnessed in the region since "the glorious days of Chief Obafemi Awolowo." (2) By way of making clear what he meant by the declaration, Aregbesola went ahead in the same document to put forward a "Six Point Integral Action Plan" which, namely, were to: 1) banish poverty, 2) banish hunger, 3) banish unemployment,

4) restore healthy living, 5) promote functional education, and 6) enhance communal peace and progress. As the then governorship candidate further declared, the six points were to be seen as "articles of faith concerning which I want to be held accountable at any time" during his tenure.

The document elaborated on each of the six points. To achieve the first one, the pledge was to revive the different commercial activities which the people in the different towns in the state had always been known for, transform Osogbo, the state capital into an "international market where goods will be procured" (p.4) at affordable prices, and promote Public/Private sector partnerships to jump start the economy." (p.5) In short, and as is made clear in the document, the overall goal of the administration would be to "reduce dependence on federal allocation" in funding programmes and projects in the state. With regards to the second point, the plan, was to boost agriculture. As was declared in the document, the situation where farmers laboured in vain would cease once the new government took over in the state. On the contrary, they would be encouraged to grow more crops in order to be able to feed the people of the state round the year. There also was a commitment to help farmers market their products and secure better storage facilities for surplus goods. Production of cash crops including cocoa and palm trees would be encouraged and farmers were to be assisted to set up cooperatives. Products when harvested would then become the basis for the establishment of micro, small and medium scale enterprises.

The third of the integral action plan focused on employment or job creation. Here, a categorical pledge was made to create 20,000 jobs within the first 100 days of the new Government in office. As further stated, 5000 of these were to be reserved for those who were laid off by the preceding administration in the state but who were still willing to work. Additionally, there was a promise to establish a Life Academy in each of the three senatorial districts of the state. The purpose of this, as stated further in the document would be to help young men and women who were no longer in schools to acquire practical skills and alternative competencies. Furthermore, it was promised to develop the state's tourism potentials in such a way that they would become sources of generating employment for the people of the state and set up "integrated industrial estates for mini, micro and large manufacturing enterprises in the three senatorial zones of Osun state." (12)

With regards to health, which is the fourth of the action plans, the projection was to establish primary health care within ten kilometre radius of every major town in the state, a general hospital within 20 kilometre radius of every community, big or small, and specialist hospitals within every 30 kilometres.

Management of environment, to PFG, constitutes a core part of any programme to ensure healthy habits. It was with regard to this that the promise was made to ensure that every home in the State of Osun had a functional toilet; and that modern, scientific method of disposing; managing and recycling wastes were introduced. It was pledged additionally to provide water for all in the state, ensure affordable housing and guarantee security of life and property.

Provision of functional education constitutes the fifth action plan. Here, and as declared in the PFG document, the vision was to put an end to the phenomenon of "frustration of youths caused by education that does not lead to employment." (16) To achieve this, the document spells out a long list of programmes which include provision of free, functional education, restoration of the dignity of the teaching professions through the introduction of incentives to teachers, re-building of all dilapidated educational structures, introduction of modern teaching aids and well-stocked libraries, encouragement of girl-child education and establishment of formal vocational training centres. In the sixth and the final plan, which was to enhance communal peace and progress, PFG declares as its mission the restoration of the trust that in the past used to exist between "the Governor and the governed." Part of what he pledged to introduce to achieve this were the establishment of the "Sages Council", the formation of "Youths Council", the launching of "Justice Sector Reforms and the establishment of "Consumer Protection Council."

The six points are intimately connected. To banish poverty, for example, people must have a means of income which may be in form of either paid employment or self employment. For the latter to be possible, the system of education must be such that makes acquisition of life-long skills possible. It is only when people are in good health that they can work consistently. And it is when and where peace reins that people can dedicate their energies to productive engagement... In other words, each of PFG's six-point agenda represents a component of a solid welfare package for the people. This is why they were described as "integral." It was why, in rounding off, the governorship candidate declared: "In all the above and above all these, I intend to run a people friendly government, a Government of the people, by the people, FOR THE PEOPLE. A GOVERNMENT UNUSUAL in this land," (emphasis original, p, 21).

Aregbesola in Office

Rauf Aregbesola achieved a decisive victory in the 2007 election. However, the People's Democratic Party (PDP), being the party in power at the national level at the time rigged the election in favour of Olagunsoye Oyinlola, its candidate in the election, and at the time the sitting governor in the state of Osun. Aregbesola immediately filed a petition with the Election Tribunal sitting in the state. The case went on for a very long time. For one, and as it became clear when the call logs between them were published in *The News*, a Nigerian newsweekly magazine, Justice Naron, the chairman of the Tribunal was in cahoots with Kunle Kalejaiye (SAN), the head of the legal team of Olagunsoye Oyinlola, in the conspiracy to pervert the course of justice. It was not surprising that when the tribunal eventually delivered judgement on the case, it was against Aregbesola, The case then went to the Appeal Court but the upper court simply returned the case to the Election Petition Tribunal sitting in the state but now composed of new judges. The "new" Tribunal still decided the case against Aregbesola. When the matter went back to it the second time, the appellate court now upturned the judgement of the Tribunal and awarded victory to Aregbesola. In all, the petition took a total of three and a half years before it was fully disposed of, but the struggle turned out to be worth it in the end.

Aregbesola was finally sworn on November 27, 2010. As soon as he came into office, he made it clear that he meant really to keep all the pledges that are contained in "My Pact." He initiated immediately a series of projects and programmes, many of them designed to impact the lives of ordinary citizens in the state. He started a credit and loan scheme, through which artisans, farmers and traders could assess loans for micro and small – scale enterprises, introduced the thirteenth month salary as a way of motivating workers in the state, rehabilitated intra-city roads, commenced work on others linking cities, towns and communities, started work on a project of re-designing and re-classification of public schools through which several schools in the state were reconstructed, introduced school feeding programmes, started the "Agba Osun", a programme through which the state provided welfare assistance to the elderly and the infirm. There also were a series of other projects with shortened names starting with letter "O" standing for Osun State. They included "O Health", the state's public health project, "O Clean", the environmental beautification project, "O Ambulance", the emergency services programme and of course, OYES, the focus of this book.

OYES: A Short Background

OYES represents the core, more or less, of number three of the six-point integral action plans. In it, and having observed that the people of the State of Osun were peaceful, hardworking men and women, PFG which Aregbesola represented avowed solemnly that as part of the "Government Unusual" type that it planned to launch as soon as it took over the rein of government in Osun, it would "create immediate employment for 20,000 people within our first 100 days in office." (7) It was pledged further that "5000 of these places shall be reserved for those who were retrenched and are still willing and able to work." (7)

Aregbesola was sworn in on November 27, 2010, only two days short of three and a half years when he was originally supposed to have taken the oath of office. Just barely twenty days (20 days) after this event, the steering committee of the Osun Youth Empowerment Scheme (OYES) had already started convening meetings. In another seventy-eight days, and precisely on March 5, 2011, a total of twenty-thousand (20,000) young men and women of the State of Osun origin were admitted into the scheme as cadets in different corps, namely Public Works Brigades, Green Gangs, Sanitation Corps, Sheriff Corps, Traffic Marshalls and Paramedics. The Teachers Corps was later to be added. They served for two years, in various areas of developmental needs of the state, and were paid ten thousand naira (N10,000) monthly. In the course of their service, many were re-trained, consequently acquiring new skills, some were absorbed as permanent staff in the State's workforce, while a number of others were sent abroad on state sponsorship to undergo one programme or the other. The scheme had general multiplier effects on all aspects of the state's economy, and took care effectively of at least the first three of the six-point integral action plan: banish poverty, banish hunger, banish unemployment through the creation of jobs. It in actual fact brought unemployment in the state down to a mere three percent (3%), making Osun the state with the lowest rate of youth unemployment in the whole of Nigeria.

OYES represented therefore an unprecedented achievement. Offering twenty thousand (20,000) jobs to people at a single instance remains unparalleled in the history of employment creation in Nigeria. Because of this, several other states in the country started contemplating the possibility of adopting the idea. Oyo, Ekiti, Kwara and Ogun were among the first set of states to contemplate the idea of introducing youth employment programmes in their different jurisdiction, modelled after that of the State of Osun. Other states like Borno and Yobe also sent people down to Osogbo to understudy the scheme's mode of operation.

The World Bank was not to take long before calling either. The global financial institution, having admitted that Osun Youth Empowerment Scheme represented the first of such initiatives anywhere in the world, took it upon itself to support the state in the efforts to keep the programme going. Additionally, it also decided to recommend it to other developing countries as a model to emulate in youth employment. In fact, the Federal Government, based on the recommendation, created a youth employment wing at the National Directorate of Employment, naming it the Youth Employment and Social Support Operation (YESSO). It was even to later introduce a sister project known as Youth Entrepreneurial Scheme (YES).

It seems clear then that OYES succeeded in inspiring a worldwide scheme in youth employment. In other words, and with OYES, what the government led by Aregbesola had done was to inaugurate a programme that would turn out to achieve global resonance. It is against this background that it was considered important to set down the details of how the programme was inaugurated, how it was run, and why it was such a success, so much so that it attracted local and global attention. This directly is the point of this book. **Apalara: Youth Employment in the State of Osun, Nigeria** records for posterity the achievements of the programme known as OYES. It delves into the origin of the programme and explores the vision that inspired it. It lays out the programme's method of recruitment, its mode of training, modalities for deployment and, as well, its impact on society. It also discusses the similarities and differences between the original version and a number of the varieties that it has inspired, including YESSO, the acronym for the one introduced by the World Bank.

The book has depended on three main sources for its materials. The first were documents that were directly inspired by the project. These included policy documents, draft bills, approved legislations, minutes of meetings of relevant committees, speeches and declarations, newspaper articles and advertisements, application and registration materials, training programmes and such other manuals, transcribed radio and television presentations, academic papers, reports by officers on the projects, and so on.

The second sources of data for the book comprised interviews that were conducted with people who had been part of the project at various levels. These included members of the implementation team including the chairman, Barrister Femi Ifaturoti, the State Coordinator, Mr. Diran Fashesin, the Commandante, Col. Eniibukun Oyewole (rtd.) who is the commander responsible for the day to day management of the project as well as deployment and logistics, and such other members as Messrs Kola Omotunde Young and Olugbenga Odulaja; consultants to the project, local government coordinators, trainers, a number of serving and former volunteers, local artisans and traders who had been involved either in supplying materials or preparing tools and kits for the cadets, and relevant officers in different Departments and Agencies of the State of Osun to which the cadets were deployed. The third source of materials was mainly the photo archives of the project collected from the commandante. Perusing the materials had required much care and consequently taken a lot of time. But it had, in the end, been quite rewarding.

It is necessary to say a word on the title of the book. The word “Apalara” is difficult to translate directly into English. In the communal worldview of the Yoruba and, indeed, most African peoples, “ara” meaning “kin” and/or “relations” represents an individual’s source of strength, protection and succour. Kin and relations are supposed to be available to bail out a person when he/she is in difficulty. “Apalara” subverts this view somewhat, insisting that true salvation lies only in the strength of an individual’s arms, in the way and manner he/she exploits his/her talents or skills. In other words, OYES did not just seek to provide temporary employment to the youths of Osun. It, on the contrary, sought to re-orientate, re-train and instil a sense of confidence in them. How far the scheme was able to achieve this will become clear in the other chapters.

CHAPTER TWO

OYES: IN THE BEGINNING

On December 1, 2010, barely four days after assuming office as the governor of the State of Osun, Aregbesola took a step that demonstrated his determination to begin to implement the pledges contained in "My Pact." Simply, he invited two of his colleagues on the PFG, namely Femi Ifaturoti and Kola Omotunde -Young and gave them the mandate to commence the process of implementing the youth employment scheme envisioned in the third integral action plan laid out in "My Pact." As should be clear in the summary of the plans included in chapter one, the focus of the third integral action plan is the provision of employment to twenty-thousand (20,000) young men and women of the state before the first hundred days in office had expired. As the governor and the two men also agreed, Gbenga Odulaja who, while not being a member of PFG, had recently started working closely with the team was also to join the implementation committee. A civil servant in the directorial cadre would be drafted to join the committee as secretary as well as the state coordinator of the scheme. The individual so appointed would also have the responsibility of ensuring that whatever decisions the implementation committee took conformed to civil service regulations. A final, important member of the committee would be the commandante, the person to be charged with the day-to-day operations of the scheme. The commandante would have to be appointed afresh and must be an individual with a military background, not lower than the rank of a colonel.

OYES was conceived as a kind of para - military scheme, sharing similarities with the National Youth Service Scheme (NYSC), except that, unlike the latter, it would be voluntary. Nonetheless, and just like the NYSC, its Chief Executive Officer would have to be a person with military experience, would take command of the orientation programme and, ultimately, supervise mobilization and deployments. He would also ensure that the cadets discharge their responsibilities in their different places of primary deployments, post orientation. It was decided to locate the project under the Ministry of Youth, Sports and Special Needs. The commandante would report to the implementation committee which in turn would report to the supervising ministry. This in turn would report to the governor. Under the commandante, there would be the Capacity Development Officer, the Logistics and Administration Officer as well as the four Liaison Officers namely; Environment and Sanitation, Security and Safety, Education and Learning and Public Works. The Capacity Development Officer was to play a supervisory role over the Directorates of Youth and Community Development officers at the local government levels while the Logistics and Administration Officer would supervise the Finance/Administration and the Technology Departments. Finally, each of the liaison officers would supervise the agencies appropriate to it at the local government levels while each of these agencies would itself supervise the volunteers posted to the Departments appropriate to it. The complete organogram is included as an appendix.

The issue of who the civil servant on the committee would be was soon to be resolved as Diran Fashesin, then a director in the Ministry of Youth, Sports and Social Needs was appointed to the position. What was left now was an officer who would serve as the commandante.

Getting an appropriate person to serve in this capacity could be described as the first major challenge the implementation committee was confronted with. The committee commenced the process by sending out announcements, and it was not long before applications started coming in. There were quite a number of them, some, in fact, from officers as high ranking as Brigadiers and Major Generals and others from those in the rank of Colonel and its equivalents. But what made that of one of the Colonels (rtd) stand out was the strong recommendation backing it up from Lt. General Alani Akinrinade (rtd).

Alani Akinrinade happens to be one of the finest and most respected military officers Nigeria has ever produced. He fought in the Nigerian civil war, and served in the capacity of Chief of Army Staff and then Chief of Defence Staff in the military government of Olusegun Obasanjo; and retired from service in the early eighties. Akinrinade is a proud indigene of Osun State, being, as it were from Ipetumodu, headquarters of Ife North Local Government, and was in the forefront of the struggles of the National Democratic Coalition (NADECO) in the late 1990s. It was well known that he nursed profound goodwill for the administration of Rauf Aregbesola. The implementation committee could not resist the pressure that a recommendation from such a person presented to it. They invited the candidate and three other officers for interaction. He himself put up a strong, impressive performance and did not waste time in accepting it when eventually he was offered the job.

The officer in question is Col. Eniibukun Oyewole (rtd). A regular combatant officer, he joined the Nigerian Army in 1973 and trained in the Nigerian Defence Academy (NDA) for two and a half years before receiving the presidential commission in 1976. Following his commission, he held several staff and command appointments in the Army and carried out special instruction activities in the Armed Forces. Colonel Oyewole (rtd) underwent staff training courses in Command and Staff College, Jaji and academic training in Florida Institute of Technology. He holds a Masters degree in Systems Management and a Master of Business Administration (MBA) degree in Logistics Management. After twenty-six years of service, Oyewole retired from the Army in 1999 to go into private business.

With Colonel Eniibukun Oyewole's (rtd) appointment as the Commandante, all was now set to start pursuing the vision embodied in Osun Youth Empowerment Scheme. OYES was conceived as a Volunteer Corps scheme, initiated in fulfilment of the pledge of the new government to put 20,000 young men and women of the state to work within its first one hundred (100) days in office. During his regular visits to the state while still a commissioner in Lagos State, Aregbesola had taken time to study the condition of existence of young men and women of the State. He had observed them as they continued to wander the streets, aimless, hopeless and literally frustrated. Though quite a significant percentage of them were well trained, they had no job and no hope of securing any. Together with his colleagues in PFG, Aregbesola had then arrived at a decision to introduce an employment scheme for the youths of the state if he succeeded in his ambition to govern it through the governorship election scheduled for May, 2007.

At the same time though, PFG was keenly aware that what had been observed in the state was replicated in virtually all other states of the federation and in several other countries. Members of People Friendly Government knew, indeed, that unemployment was/is a global problem. They therefore had a twin aim for the scheme they wanted to launch in Osun. In the first place, it was their primary desire to put the young people of the state to work, engage them productively and make them develop a sense of self-worth. The stipend they would be paid at the end of each month would represent only a basic earning, clearly something to look forward to, and which they could struggle to add to through other forms of engagement. In essence, by introducing OYES, the administration's aim was to fire the imaginations of the beneficiaries and train them to explore their latent potentials and talents, and transform same into skills with which to keep them continuously productive after they must have been disengaged from the scheme. This way, they would have become self empowered, imbibed the spirit of self-dependence, understood the meaning of hard work, commitment to self and communal well-being, and appreciated what is meant by dignity of labour.

The second aim which Aregbesola's administration hoped to achieve through OYES was to create a scheme of employment that would represent a model to other states and indeed other countries in different parts of the world which equally experience problems of acute shortage of means of livelihood for their teeming youths. Such other states and, as the case might be, countries, could then adopt the Osun template and modify it to suit their own specific situations. Against this larger aim, Aregbesola and his colleagues in PFG knew that there were great challenges on the way. Indeed, for any outsider to feel convinced that the programme was worthy of emulation, it had to be seen that those who were benefiting from the scheme were those who absolutely need employment. Secondly, there had to be demonstrated transparency in the handling of the finances attaching to all aspects of the scheme. This second point was important, especially given the country's frightening reputation for corruption and graft. But the government had trusted hands on the implementation committee, with at least two of them being those the governor himself had worked with for a long time, actually members of PFG, the driving force behind the new government.

But there were other issues which the governor thought the implementation committee ought to take on board while working out the details of the scheme. One was how to ensure that the benefits of the scheme percolated down, that whatever funds were invested in it benefited not just the volunteers but rather circulated within the state such that the ordinary run of the citizenry would also have a feel of its positive impact. The second issue has already been hinted at. It has to do with how to build long term benefits into the programme. The question, in other words bothered on how to upgrade whatever skills a beneficiary possessed before enlisting on the scheme, or get him/her acquire one afresh if he/she possessed none originally. This was all in order that they might be able to continue to utilize such skills for personal sustenance even after they might have graduated from the scheme. Third, the state also had areas of needs, areas where it did not yet have sufficient manpower. The question was posed then as to whether, if it was discovered that some of those who enlisted as volunteers had talents relevant to these special areas, it would not be appropriate to tap such and use them to take care of such needs. Related to this were those who had latent potentials, innate qualities that needed to be brought out into the open. It was thought that when discovered, the state ought to, as resources permitted, assist in developing such endowments by offering them scholarships for further training either locally or even beyond the shores of the country. Finally, there was the issue of certifying that participants worked for the stipend that they received while on the scheme while at the same time ensuring that they had sufficient time left for them to expend on other sources of income.

II

The Implementation Committee took all these issues into consideration while working out the details of the scheme. Eventually, it came up with a twenty – four month revolving scheme, which would keep the twenty thousand volunteers in temporary employment for the set duration, disengaging them once the period lapsed and enlisting new ones immediately after. The age range of would-be volunteers was set at between 18 and 35 years. To qualify, an individual must be a citizen of Osun State and possess a minimum educational qualification of West African School Certificate. The Management Committee was quite flexible in its interpretation of who qualified as a citizen of the state. As Colonel Oyewole (rtd) explained to this writer in an interview, a person whose parents were not originally from Osun, but had otherwise resided in the state continuously for the three years immediately preceding the time of filing his/her application, and had never defaulted in paying taxes would not be discriminated against in the process of selection once he/she happened to possess the requisite qualifications.

With regards to remuneration, a volunteer's allowance was fixed at ten thousand naira per month (N10, 000). The amount was considered substantial enough for the volunteer to look forward to at the end of each month, representing, as it were, a source of basic income, meant to be used to meet only important needs. While the amount fell just within what the state economy could afford, it was also deliberately cut low so as to prevent a beneficiary from thinking of spending part of it on matters of pleasure; like, for example, a holiday or weekend outside the state. In other words, the scheme was designed in such a way that a large chunk of the allowance paid to volunteers - if not the entire sum - would circulate within the state economy, likely to be spent as it were on foodstuff, transportation, rents, children school fees, etc. It is probably better to allow the commandante, Colonel Oyewole (rtd) express this logic in his own words:

> Let me illustrate the thinking behind the ten thousand naira that we pay our cadets. Will anybody that is paid ten thousand naira go for a party in Lagos at weekend? He will not! How is he likely to spend his ten thousand naira? He is going to spend it on the basic needs on his Maslow hierarchy of needs. The Maslow hierarchy of needs focuses on the basic needs of life: provide for what you eat, what you drink, where you sleep, what you wear for (protection against the elements)…for these rudimentary things. It is these needs of our cadets that we are concerned to cater for. And where are they likely to spend the allowance? Here, in the respective local governments in which they are engaged.

"Let's make sure the money we pay them does not leave the state" – that seems to be what members of the Implementation Committee of OYES told themselves while trying to figure out what would be appropriate as monthly remunerations. Ten thousand naira in twenty thousand places translates to two hundred million naira (N200 million). This at least was the amount that would be injected into the economy of the State of Osun each month through allowances paid to volunteer cadets alone, and from which the people residing there would benefit. Two hundred million naira in twelve months translates to 2.4 billion naira. This again was what the scheme contributed to the resources that circulated within the state each year. The amount could exactly not be described as fantastic but it was still considerable, especially when the fact was considered that the sources of income of the state in question are almost severely limited.

As regards mode of payment, it was decided to adopt the method of direct bank transfers to the individual accounts of the volunteers. The

Implementation Committee thought it would be neat to get all of them to have an account each in one single bank. Following stiff competition to get the account by financial institutions, and also because it donated a princely sum of one hundred million naira (N100m) to the state government in support of the programme, First Bank was selected for this purpose. So, at the end of every month, the supervising ministry would pay the allowances for all the volunteers in bulk to the bank, and the latter in turn would credit the account of each of them with the designated amount. The method allowed no room for any kind of temptation as none of the officers charged with implementing the programme, not even the commandante, would by so doing have any opportunity to come in direct contact with the scheme's funds.

But since the amount being paid the volunteers was cut so low, deliberately designed as it were to meet only their basic needs, it was clear that they would also need to be allowed to have time that could be spent on other means of income. To this end, the Implementation Committee decided to make most of the deployments last only from seven o clock to ten or eleven o clock in the morning, making it four hours a day, at most, on Monday till Friday. From the time they would be released till the end of the day, volunteers remained on their own; free to engage in things that would fetch them further income. Again, here is the sense that Oyewole, the commandante, makes of it:

> Of course, I trust you will bear me witness Professor Raji. Those of us who studied overseas, we worked at two, three, or even four places at the same time – certainly on a minimum of two jobs to make ends meet. And I know how people used to quickly pull off the uniforms they used on a job they had just left, put on the one that is appropriate to the ones they wanted to move on to… or even snatch one hour of sleep before they resume at the next job. So we let our cadets know this. We tell them that when we release them at ten, it is not for them to go home saying, mo ti sise oni tan sic. No, the day's work has not finished. Each volunteer must find something else to do. Now, if I paid a kid 10 thousand Naira for four hours and he is able to do another four hours from ten to two o clock, and he makes another 10 thousand naira, how much will that come to?

The Implementation Committee also decided to build a three – week orientation programme into the beginning of each set of the revolving scheme. As it happens with NYSC from which the Committee did, in this regard, derive some inspiration, all volunteers were expected to spend the period together in a camp undergoing training. The details of what the training consisted of will be the focus of chapter three. But, briefly, as is usual with such training, there were to be physical drills, detailed explanations of the code of conduct for the trainees, rudimentary lessons in computer, tips on health and safety at work, issues on work ethics, lessons on how to choose a career and drills on effective communications. There also were topics on indigenous cultural values, especially the ethics of "omoluabi", Yoruba word for a well trained, well bred and well behaved individual and, as well, the history and economic system of Nigeria as a country and the challenges this present to ordinary people.

Cadets were to be posted to their places of primary assignment immediately on conclusion of the training programme. For the first three months, it was decided that all volunteers should be deployed to participate in street cleaning exercise, if they were females, or trimming of verges, if they were males. Afterwards, each volunteer would then be posted to anyone of seven areas that was approximate to his/her field of competence. Here is how Diran Fashesin, the state coordinator describes the different fields into which cadets could be deployed:

> The cadets shall be deployed to various locations as determined by the government and each deployment shall be provided with distinct uniforms and accessories. The deployment shall include but not limited to Public Works, Paramedics and Sheriff Corps, Teachers squad (sic), Sanitation Czars, Green Gang, Civil Service, Traffic Marshal

Deployment will be discussed in details in chapter four. Suffice it at this point to state that it was decided to have uniforms for the volunteers. To this end, it was further decided to issue each volunteer with two sets of these uniforms, a set of boots and simple working implements such as rakes, cutlasses, brooms, brushes, scissors, nose covers, hand gloves, work suits made of khaki, cutlasses, wheel barrows, iron-rakes, blade files, reflector jackets and security boots at the point of inauguration. Again, consistent with the practice of ensuring that any funds invested on the scheme circulated within the economy of the state, materials used in sewing the uniforms were purchased from local cloth sellers, the sewing itself done by local tailors, the logo on the uniform designed by local artisans, the supply of boots sourced to local cobblers, and working implements procured from local traders. Chapter five will be devoted to the testimonies of some of these secondary beneficiaries of the scheme.

III

But I shouldn't give the impression that the Implementation Committee had a lot of time to work out a plan for the scheme prior to when the programme took off. To the new government, that was some form of luxury that could not be tolerated at the time. It happened, actually, that the Committee had to think on its feet, working out, as it were, a blueprint for the scheme even as it carried on with the process of recruitment. The urgency was dictated by the fact that the governor had pledged to create 20,000 jobs for unemployed youths within his first one hundred days in office and was determined to keep his word.

It has earlier been pointed out that he was only four days old in office when he gave Femi Ifaturoti and Kola Omotunde -Young the mandate to commence the process of the implementation of the employment scheme that would later come to be known as OYES. At that time, the governor had not even moved into his office in Abere, Osogbo, or his official residence in GRA. He was in fact operating from somewhere in Ilesa. The process of change of signatories had not been concluded so the new government had no access as yet to funds. Nobody, with the probable exception of Chief of Staff, had as yet been formally appointed into office. What this meant was that members of the implementation committee could not even be issued letters of appointment before being asked to embark on the assignment given to them. But since it was originally a joint dream, the team was more than ready – if this kind of expression could be permitted – to start working as at the time the governor gave them the directive.

So, together, Femi Ifaturoti, Kola Omotunde - Young, Gbenga Odulaja, and Diran Fashesin set to work. By December 17, 2010, the process of recruitment of the first set of volunteers had commenced. Announcements went out, asking qualified and interested candidates to start collecting application forms. The announcements were placed on both the radio and television services of the Osun State Broadcasting Corporation (OSBC) as well as Unique FM, Ilesa. Adverts were also placed in national newspapers just as posters and handbills were printed and circulated. Interested candidates were instructed to collect application forms - which were free of charge - from their respective local governments of origin, complete and submit them through the same channels. One of the handbills was titled "Apalara" and it blared out the following:

For the purpose of coordinating the exercise, the office of the Head of Service had actually released 31 officers, deploying one to each of the 30 local government areas and Ife-East Area Office. Collection of application forms commenced on December 20, 2010.

Underestimating the level of unemployment in the state, the implementation committee decided to print only 100,000 application forms initially. These were exhausted within three days. The next 50,000 forms delivered on December 25 got finished in less than 36 hours. By this time, the implementation committee had arrived at a full understanding of the reality of the level of unemployment, not just in the state but in the country as a whole. It was decided to print 100,000 forms more to make a total of 250,000. At a point, allegations of hoarding of application forms started being levied against politicians and civil servants. To address this, what the implementation committee did was to create a website (oyes.org.ng) for the new scheme and put the form on it. This made the application to be freely available for all interested individuals to download. The approach effectively removed the artificial barriers being created against accessing applications.

The original deadline for collection of application forms was December 24, 2010. In view of the need to be fair to those who had difficulty obtaining the forms, the deadline was extended to January 7, 2011.

In the process of sorting out the applications, members of the implementation committee discovered that response to the call for applications was good across all the local government areas in the state. Saying this however is not the same thing as suggesting that the percentage of response was, in general, even. In fact, while, for example, the advertisement recorded heavy responses in local governments like Osogbo and Olorunda, relatively much fewer people sent in applications from small and sparsely populated ones like Oriade. But right from the onset, the committee had decided to make sure that people from all parts of the state benefited from the scheme.

Preliminary screening was done using biometric data which included age, gender, qualifications, local government areas and working experience. Candidates who could not present evidence of having ever attempted the West African School Certificate Examination or its equivalent were all disqualified. There had to be a baseline.

The preliminary exercise only succeeded in reducing the applications by about fifty thousand. Given this reality, what the implementation committee did was to work out a percentage of the applicants that it could accommodate as volunteers in the first set. Since, for example, it now had about 200,000 applications as against 20,000 slots it had to fill, the committee decided to make ten percent (10%) the average of the applications that would be approved from each of the local governments. But again, given the fact that the rate of subscription was not the same across local governments, it also became clear to the committee that it could not simply apply the average across board, that the principle of affirmative action had to be applied, somewhat. Thus it happened that for places like Osogbo, Olorunda, Ife Central, Ilesa East and Ilesa West, the average was cut down to about eight percent – in fact, in one or two cases, six or seven percent. On the other hand, and in a number of local governments from where there were not too many applications, the average was jerked up. In the case of Oriade, almost all qualified candidates were mopped up. It was a strenuous, painstaking exercise but the implementation committee had no choice than to follow it through for the sake of fairness, and because of the need to win public trust and confidence for the scheme.

Training commenced as soon as decisions on enlistments had been concluded. The original plan was to conduct the training in one single, central location but the implementation committee would soon discover that there was no place large enough in the entire state that could accommodate such a large number. Eventually, it was decided to decentralize the exercise, and the training now took place in all the thirty (30) local government areas and Ife East Area office. A two – day Train-the-Trainer workshop was first organized for those who would carry out the training on February 1 – 2, 2011. Volunteer Cadets' training course itself took place between February 4 and 22. The first day was devoted to registration, collection of kits and basic medical check-ups. Two days after, all cadets were paid a training allowance of eight thousand naira (N8000) each. At the end of the exercise, those who were adjudged to have conformed with the code of conduct of the training were issued with what was termed "Letter of Engagement." The letter informed the addressee that

> following your successful application, selection and completion of the mandatory training course… the OYES Secretariat is pleased to inform you of your engagement as a member of OYES Volunteer Cadet…

The final paragraph of the letter made it clear that the offer was "provisional" and shall become valid only upon receipt of a written letter of acceptance of offer in your own hand written (sic) within 7 working days of receipt of this letter." Thus began a programme that would soon become a model of youth empowerment for many countries, even for World Bank, the world number one financial institution; and which was to automatically reduce the rate of unemployment in Osun state from 11 percent to a mere 3 percent. I intend to write further on this point in the concluding chapter.

CHAPTER THREE

TRAINING

Training programme in OYES lasted for three weeks and took place in centres so designated in each of the 30 local government areas and Ife East Area office of the state. Unlike what obtains in NYSC, it was non-residential. Rather, participants were required to report from home on a daily basis. They arrived in the morning and returned home at the close of session each day. For the very first batch, training took place from February 4 – 22, 2011. Training for the second batch on the other hand was held between February 11 and 28, 2013. Engineer Abimbola Daniyan and Comrade Abiodun Aremu were engaged for the purposes of coordinating the programme. In one of the power point presentations used at the Train-the-Trainers workshop held on February 1-2, 2011, the mission statement of the programme was presented in the following words:

> To enable trainees to gain the knowledge and practical skills, and imbibe the values and work ethic of **Apalara Ise l'ewa** Osun (the beauty of Osun land derives from the people's labour).
>
> To build the trainees into worthy OYES Volunteer Corps members who are fit (morally, mentally and physically)

> and committing their capabilities to improving the people's quality of life with integrity, efficiency and humility, as becoming of **Omoluabi** (honourable persons), **the embodiment of Oranyan's ideals**.

The guiding philosophy, on the other hand, was presented as follows:

> To inculcate in the trainees the right attitude and competence in the tasks and techniques essential for efficient, qualitative and safe delivery of service to Osun people, cognisant of the people's glorious history, rich culture and high ideals and yearning for renewal, by adopting appropriate technological and management tools and solutions.

In essence, the mission and philosophy of the training programme was consistent with the original vision which gave birth to the establishment of the Osun Youth Empowerment Scheme (OYES), this being to guide the young people of the state in their struggles to eliminate frustrations and sense of despair engendered by unemployment and lack of fulfilment. The training was supposed to represent the foundation, a solid one at that, upon which the cadets would build their hopes.

Right from this point, they were supposed to begin to acquire business-oriented skills as well as vocational, technical and professional competence.

The application and screening processes which had already been treated in chapter two was followed by publication of names of successful applicants on the internet. The names were actually published on a portal specially created for OYES and sorted to local governments. Those who then found their names on the Internet were directed to report at the designated training centres - where the names were also displayed. This was deliberately so designed to manage crowd. In fact, there was a further advice for those who did not find their names on the internet to stay away from the training centres.

Applicants were directed to these centres to find out if they were successful. Those who found their names were instructed to check and record their OYES codes as it was this that would enable them proceed to the next stage which, basically, consisted of screening of credentials as well as basic medical and physical fitness checks.

Screening simply entailed ascertaining the authenticity of the credentials which the candidates submitted along with their applications. For this purpose, each would-be cadet was asked to produce the originals of the documents. Once a candidate scaled through this stage, he/she was directed to the next section where his/her weights and heights were measured and duly recorded. Following this, he/she would then be ushered to the place where orientation kits were collected. Kits simply comprised t-shirt, a pair of shorts, a face cap, a pair of stockings and white tennis shoes. This was all that was done for the first day. Following it, trainees were discharged and instructed to report the following day at six in the morning.

Volunteer cadets' training schedule for 2011 and 2013 basically consisted of physical training and lessons taken in classroom context. The schedule for 2011 showed that the day that followed the one when trainees underwent registration and collected their kits was devoted to road walk. This was Saturday February 5. The next day, being Sunday, was apparently left free as the schedule did not record anything for it. The three days from Monday February 7, to Wednesday February 9 were equally devoted to physical training. The first set of lessons were held on Thursday 10th and Friday, 11th. On Saturday 12th, cadets returned to physical training.

Monday 14th to Thursday 17th were devoted to lectures and team building exercise. Cadet trainees returned to physical exercises on Friday 18th, and this was rounded off finally on Saturday 19th. Lectures were themselves rounded off on Monday February 21. The second half of that day was devoted to what was described as "working tools demonstration." Here the tools which the cadets would be using in their different places of deployment were displayed, and how to use each of them, demonstrated. The final day, Tuesday, February 22 was devoted wholly to socials and entertainment.

As Adetokunbo Shittu, a cadet in the 2011 – 2013 batch revealed, the first day of training started at about 6.45 am with the introduction of officials who would be in charge of the different aspects of the programme. The cadets were then split into platoons and taken through routine physical training. That went on for about one hour. After this, they were introduced to rudiments of military parade, made to learn basic military etiquettes and respect for hierarchies as regards relations to one's colleagues and superiors. This was shortly followed by parade rehearsals in which the cadets were prepared for the inauguration that was to come up three weeks later. This went on till about 10.00am when they were allocated to lecture halls in accordance with their OYES registration codes. At about 4:00 p.m. the day's activities were declared closed.

The next day started with routine exercises and parade rehearsals, again as Shittu submitted. At 10.00am, trainees were ordered to proceed to their various halls where lectures and orientation proper commenced. It turned out to be a three-week process of close intellectual rapport between the trainees and the facilitators who took them through a well structured programme based on the pre-designed module; in a classroom setting. The trainees were each given a package consisting of a branded file holder, containing the OYES module, a writing pad, a pen and a pencil.

Following registration, perhaps the very first thing the cadets were taken through were the rules and regulations guiding the training. These were otherwise described as the trainees' code of conduct. This was very elaborate, divided as it were into twenty – one (21) sub-sections. Directly, the headings of the sub sections respectively are Guiding/Core Values, Core Objective, Discipline, Registration, General Conduct, Attendance & Punctuality, Respect for Nation & State, Respect for People, Prohibited Items, Classroom & Field Conduct, Use of Mobile Phones, Responsible Behaviour, Attire & Appearance, Rules & Regulations, Conduct & Attitude, Attendance, Missed Classes & Tardiness, Leave of Absence, Release from Training & Cadetship, Probation, Re-admittance and finally, Condition for Award of Cadet Certificate . I think it is better to simply reproduce what is articulated under each of the sub-sections unedited:

CORE VALUES

Honesty, Integrity, Discipline, Hard Work, Safety, Competence, Quality, Efficiency, Respect for all, Oneness, Leadership and Loyalty.

CORE OBJECTIVE OF THE TRAINING PROGRAMME

The core objective of the OYES Volunteer Cadets' Training Programme [OYESVCTP] is to lay a solid foundation for a brighter future for the youths of Osun State, through the impartation of business-oriented vocational, technical and professional skills and attitude.

REGISTRATION

On arrival at the premises for the Training Programme each Trainee Cadet shall report at the Administration Office, and shall fill the Trainee Cadet's Registration Form. The completed Form shall be submitted to the Admin Office and be recorded in the Trainee Reception Register for the issuance of a Welcome Kit. Upon completion of the registration exercise all Trainees shall assemble at the designated Muster Point(s) where they shall be briefed on the Medical Fitness Procedure and provided with details of the facilities and services for their convenience during the period of their training. Trainee's admission to the Programme is formalised by registration in the Administration/Academic Office of the Programme, that is, by obtaining and completing correctly and truthfully all the required information on the Admission Registration Form supplied in the Trainee Welcome Kit. The forms shall be completed and returned to the Admin/Academic Office on or before 10.00hours. Information provided will be scrutinised and verified for accuracy and completeness by the Programme Administration Office.

DISCIPLINE

All trainees are required to obey the Rules and Regulations contained in this Code of Conduct. Trainee Cadets are considered as Ambassadors of Goodwill for the Programme, as such, their performances and behaviours will be used to gauge both the Trainee Cadets and the Programme. Each Trainee Cadet is required to develop personal discipline and maintain good order within and outside the training sites, by obeying the rules set out in this code of conduct in order to earn a good reputation for themselves and the Programme. Safety and Security Rules are meant to help develop in the trainees and Programme personnel a positive safety and security culture. Disciplinary and safety rules constitute keys to your eventual career success.

The Programme's vision for discipline is to guide and motivate Trainee Cadets towards exemplary conduct in support of teaching and learning, during the training, and coaching and mentoring on the job assignments. The enforcement of the training rules and regulations aims to provide a safe and conducive environment, correct misbehaviour and ensure that trainees learn from their mistakes, and graduate to become highly professionally skilled Cadets and respectable citizens. Defaulters shall face the Programme Disciplinary Procedures and will be appropriately sanctioned.

ATTENDANCE AND PUNCTUALITY

Attend classes and other training activities punctually. Skipping any of them will be treated as truancy and indiscipline cases. Late coming is prohibited. Absence from any training activities must be by written formal permission of the Administrative Lead (in consultation with Admin Head) or substantiated by a Medical Report

PROHIBITED ITEMS

The following items are considered injurious to the objectives of the Programme, and on no account shall a trainee possess, keep or use them.

Pornographic materials

Weapons

Pyrotechnics

Tobacco products and alcohol

Gambling and gaming devices of all descriptions.

Poker cards or tiles

All items that the Programme Authority deems to be potentially offensive, disruptive or harmful

All other items prohibited under Nigerian law

RESPECT FOR NATION AND STATE

All trainees are to observe the flag raising and lowering ceremonies with dignity and respect.

All Trainees shall sing the National Anthem and recite the Pledge.

All trainees are to sing the **OYES Anthem** and recite the **Trainee Creed** respectfully.

Proper decorum (**iwa omoluabi**) must be observed during all assemblies and functions.

All trainees must uphold the reputation of the Programme and the dignity of the nation at all times. For example there must be no defamation (in any form) of the Programme or any staff of the Programme.

Trainees are to show respect to all Officials of the Programme and visitors when they meet them.

RESPONSIBLE BEHAVIOUR

Trainees are expected to keep the classroom and workshop facilities and tools neat, presentable and clean at all times.

No food items are allowed in the classrooms.

All food items must be consumed in the designated canteen area.

Only plain water can be brought to the classroom.

Trainees' personal effects are not to be left in the classroom after training hours

ATTIRE AND APPEARANCE

Trainees are to wear the prescribed Programme uniforms.

Trainee uniform as shown in the student handbook must be worn – shorts, trousers, shirts, and T-shirts must be tucked in at all times.

Trainees are to wear the correct PPEs. Proper Programme training shoes should be worn. Trainees who are unable to comply due to injury are to see the Discipline Master personally for an excuse slip before the morning assembly.

Only the OYES uniforms may be worn over a shirt.

RULES & REGULATIONS

The aims of establishing the Programme Rules & Regulations and Trainee Code of Conduct are to foster self-discipline and good behaviour and to maintain a good learning environment.

The Programme Regulations are applicable to all trainees. This Regulation is also applicable to trainees wearing Programme colours and insignia outside premises and those participating in extracurricular activities on behalf of the school.

All trainees are expected to observe regulations, take care of the facilities, respect tutors, care for Course mates, keep good discipline, study diligently, be serious, honest, responsible, thrifty, polite and neat in appearance and be enthusiastic in service.

ACCOMMODATION:

There will be no provision for accommodation. The lecture halls, conveniences, etc shall be used in a way and manner that promotes harmony and orderly living.

GENERAL CONDUCT

Maintain decorum at all times

Respect and obey the programme authorities

Be polite to others. Do not hurt others regardless of circumstances

Take good care of programme's properties

Demonstrate a sense of civic mindedness

Trainees are to promptly attend for activities

Trainees are to be well behaved during programmes

CLASSROOM CONDUCT:

Trainee must respect their tutors during and after classes, they must do assignments, they must not bring food to classes, only water is allowed and their personal effects are not to be left in the classrooms after training hours.

USE OF MOBILE PHONES IN SCHOOL:

Trainees may bring mobile phones to the class, but must obey all relations attached to it. They must take full responsibility for the safety of their mobile phones and use of mobile phones should not disrupt any programme or activity being conducted

CONDUCT AND ATTITUDE:

Trainee should not be impaired by alcohol or illegal drugs while on campus. Trainees and staff work as a team to assist one another to reach excellence. A trainee may be dismissed for any illegal activities.

ATTENDANCE MISSED CLASSES AND TARDINESS:

Instructors have the right to deduct points from assignments that are submitted late. Make-up work may be allowed. A trainee will be given the opportunity to fulfil missed course work or homework, when possible.

LEAVE OF ABSENCE:

A trainee may be given leave of absence in case of emergencies and family problems. The trainee must return within the stipulated time, if not, the trainee's contract may be terminated.

RELEASE FROM TRAINING PROGRAMME:

The circumstances of which a trainee may be released from programme are:

(I) indulgence in acts of gross misconduct in violation of the programme rules and regulations,

(ii) a failure to make the required pass mark of 50%.

CONDITIONS FOR OBTAINING THE OYES CERTIFICATE OF ATTENDANCE

A Certificate of Attendance is to be awarded to each trainee upon successful completion of the Programme. Successful Completion is conditional upon good conduct and good academic and practical performance.

PROBATION:

A trainee that does not adhere to the attendance policy will be placed on probation. If the trainee has not corrected the attendance problem within three days, the trainee will be counselled by the administrative office, with a possibility of release from the programme

RE-ENTRY:

A trainee whose attendance has been terminated may not be allowed to re-enter the programme, except in special circumstances.

The code of conduct was no doubt elaborate and detailed and made clear the organisers' sense of mission, the importance attached to the training programme and the seriousness with which beneficiaries were expected to take it. The Yoruba word "apalara" was central to the objective of the course. As has been explained in chapter one, the word was intended to make the cadets believe that their "arms" represent the best and the closest of all kin and relations. Only the strength of an individual's arms, and nothing else, could raise him/her up, and rescue him/her from hunger, poverty and want. In other words, a sense of purpose, an attitude of independence and a feeling of self determination represented, beyond everything else, the core values which the brains behind the scheme would like the cadet trainees to cultivate. Beyond being an important Yoruba word, "Apalara" is also the title of a poem – actually a rhyme - written in the same language presumably by J.F. Odunjo, one of the best known Yoruba language poets and, arguably, the most successful of all authors of Yoruba language school texts... Flowing from its title, the poem itself represents a kind of philosophical admonition to young people. It used to be a popular fare in primary schools in the 60's, 70's and early 80's. Its message, simply, is that success can be achieved only through hard work, persistence and perseverance. I think it is better to reproduce the poem in full and then provide a rough English translation of it:

Apalara (By J.F.Odunjo)

Ise l'oogun Ise
Mura si'se ore mi,
Ise la fi nd'eni giga
Ti a ko ba r'eni fehinti, bi ole laa ri
Bi a ko ba r'eni gbekele, a te'ra mo'se ni
Iya re lee l'owo l'owo,
Baba re lee l'esin lekan
Bi o ba gboju le won, O te tan ni mo so fun o
Iya n be f'omo ti ko gbon,
Ekun n be f'omo ti nsa kiri
Mo f'owuro se're ore mi
Mura si'se ojo n lo.

My translation goes thus:

Hard work represents the only effective remedy against poverty
Work hard, dear friend
Only hard work makes a person great
One who has nobody to lean on always looks indolent
One who has none to depend on should simply lean on him/herself
Your mother may possess an ocean of wealth
And your father, vast stables of horses
You'll still not succeed, should you cast your hopes on them
He who ignores wise counsel will suffer greatly
He who fails to learn will shed tears of regret.
Joke not with the early period of a day
Work very hard, dear friend.

Being so rough, the translation might not have conveyed the full sense of the Yoruba original but it should still make clear the idea it was trying to drive across. Hard work, self dependence, a sense of mission, great vision are central messages the poem tries to make sure any reader did not miss. And all of them were central to the goals of OYES. It was for this reason that recitation of the poem was made integral to the lessons delivered during the training. Adetokunbo Shittu attested to how trainees were made to learn the poem by heart, and how it was recited during almost all lessons, with each recitation followed by short discussion sessions, obviously in an effort to ensure that the trainees understood its contents and internalised them.

The component of the course concerned with physical fitness attained its peak on the day the governor, Ogbeni Rauf Aregbesola, joined the cadets posted to Osogbo and Olorunda Local Governments areas in endurance walk round the city of Osogbo. The endurance walk, by the way, was a state-wide event during which cadets took off from designated places in their different local government headquarters and walked to some other designated places under the direction of their mentors, officials and other well wishers.

For Osogbo and Olorunda, all the cadet trainees were instructed to report at St. Charles Grammar School, the training venue for the two local government areas, for the event. In addition to the governor, all the OYES officials including the commandante, other members of the OYES Implementation Committee participated in the exercise, and so did the commandants of all military and paramilitary agencies in the state. The procession, which started at St. Charles Grammar School, Osogbo, passed through Ita-Olookan to Station Road. Then turning left towards Oke-Fia at Old Garage, the group went through Alekuwodo and, at Olaiya junction, turned right to face Gbongan road. The cadets stopped when they got to Oranyan House. Here they were addressed by Governor Aregbesola and consequently dismissed for the day.

The walk generated much excitement, not just among cadet trainees but also among the people of the town. They in fact trooped out in large number to cheer the Governor and his retinue of excited youths, who all appeared to be unaffected by the cold harmattan winds. Of course, ambulances followed the procession, ready, as they were, to take care of any emergencies or give ride to participants who might at any point feel exhausted.

The lecture series, being the second component of the course covered seven key areas. Actually, only four of these were taken in the 2011 exercise, with the other three added in 2013. The first topic was broad and general and seeks to provide explanations on how our people and society came to be at the point where they currently were. Its title was equally broad: "History, Culture, Economics, Law and Politics: The Reasons we are Here." The second topic was on communication and its title was both simple and direct: "Effective Communications: Making Yourself Understood." The third focuses on issues of health, safety and security at work and was again given a title that boldly announced its concern: "Health and Safety at Work." The last of the ones treated in 2011 was on how to understand oneself, one's abilities and peculiar psychological traits. It was titled "Know Yourself and why You Are Here: Attitude and Skills for the Model OYES Cadet." The topics were each given out to an expert who prepared lesson notes on them. The lesson notes were later compiled, published in form of modules and given out to the trainees at the beginning of the course. It was in 2013 that the module was revised and expanded to include such topics as "Democracy in Nigeria", "Workplace Psychology", "Differences between Rich and Poor Countries" and finally "Positioning Oneself for Opportunities."

It is probably necessary to provide a brief outline of each of the topics as a way of shedding light on what the coordinators of the course tried to impart to the cadet trainees. "History, Culture, Economics, Law and Politics: The Reasons we are Here" was prepared by Laoye Sanda of the Ola Oni Labour Education Research Centre, Ibadan. Issues discussed under the topic include the relevance of history as a subject, evolution of human society, how culture developed, material and abstract dimensions of culture, African origin of civilization, key points in Nigeria history, concepts of production, distribution and exchange, colonial and neo-colonial exploitation, socialist theory of economic development, laws of social transformation, the necessity of change and, finally, how the OYES programme represented a positive step in the process of change. The second topic which was titled "Effective Communications: Making Yourself Understood" was anchored by Abimbola Daniyan. The sub-topics covered under it included forms of communications, effective communication at the place of work, barriers to communication, verbal and non-verbal communications, facts, feelings and purpose in communications, questions and their types, conflicts and how to overcome them, and processes of taking sound decisions. "Health and Safety at Work", being the third topic was also handled by Abimbola Daniyan. Its scope was wide and included occupational health and hygiene, fitness for work, with the key word defined as the ability to cope with both the physical and psychological demands of an individual's job, different kinds of occupational hazards and how to avoid or prevent them, substances that constitute hazard to health and how to control them, working in confined spaces and regulations guiding them, noise, noise levels and regulations relating to noise at work, first aid, response in emergency situation, alcoholism and drug abuse, the work environment, housekeeping at work, security and security consciousness at work, accidents and accident prevention, causes of accidents, safe operations, and list of common hazards.

The fourth topic was titled "Know Yourself and why You are Here: Attitude and Skills for the Model OYES Cadet." This one began by foregrounding the concept of "omoluabi", the Yoruba word for a person of good morality, great ethical standing, integrity and self worth. Actually, in addition to "apalara", the word "omoluabi" was the other Yoruba word that was made central to OYES training programme. Cadets were in fact admonished, again and again, to strive toward internalizing its core tenets. Other issues raised under this topic included the importance of getting one's priority right, the question of self discipline, why it is important to master English language, personality and behaviour, different types of personality traits, and what was described as the seven habits that make effective people.

The topic "Democracy in Nigeria" was culled from the training manual of the Institute for Development and Democratic Studies (IDDS), and focused on such issues as the concept of democracy, Nigeria's experience in Democracy, core values of Democracy and institutions of democracy. "Workplace Psychology" being the fifth topic, was concerned essentially with conflict, conflict management strategies, team building, team versus group, team versus traditional organization, group behaviour, and how to establish trust. The next topic titled "Differences between Rich and Poor Countries" was anchored by Kola Omotunde - Young. In this lecture, Omotunde Young drew comparison between rich and poor countries giving reasons why some were poor, and others, rich. He concluded it by asking people to stop the blame game but rather develop an attitude of self focus. As he put it, it was only through this that a process of change could commence. The last topic titled "Positioning yourself for Opportunities" was also handled by Kola Omotunde Young. Some of the points raised in it included desire for success, positioning oneself for success, fundamental requirements for success, dangers of procrastination, and the need to save and invest in the future.

As can be seen from the summary of the contents of the lectures, OYES training programme sought to develop the trainee's body, mind and intellect; the body through physical drills; and the mind and intellect through the lessons. The general learning series, as it was called, had the aim of making the cadet trainees discover who they were, learn to communicate effectively, understand other people and how to team up with them, know their society's history, culture and economic structure, discover opportunities it offers and learn how to tap them, gain basic knowledge of health and safety issues and in general develop skills that can make them independent and achieve self fulfilment.

Built into the programme were measures aimed at testing and evaluating how effective the lessons had been, and how well the trainees had followed them. Again Adetokunbo Shittu reports that, at the end of the first week, after the topic on team work and effective communication had been taught, the trainees were divided into groups of tens, with each group given an assignment to prepare a seminar presentation on a chosen topic. Such topics included democracy, bribery and corruption, and unemployment. Says Shittu: "the most successful groups were awarded points which at the end of the training translated to various forms of rewards."

And in the third week, a general test was given to all the course participants. The test signalled the end of official lectures and group work sessions, and its purpose was to discover how much knowledge the participants had gained in the course of the training. It was, in fact, made clear to the trainees that their deployment to places of primary assignment would depend on their performances in the examination. With this, everybody took it seriously. Trainees prepared well for the test and the trainers made sure it was closely supervised. Pass mark was fixed at fifty percent (50%). As it turned out, more than 98% of those who participated in the test made the pass grade.

Another major event that was organized before the close of training was the OYES talent hunt show. This was made part of the social event with which the programme wound up. At this point, I would like to quote Shittu's own words as he struggles to bring back what this actually consists of:

> People were encouraged to register and present artistic works in a hotly contested competition which had rewards for the first three top contenders. The second runner up was to go home with a certificate of participation while the first runner up went away with both a certificate and a cash price of about 5000 Naira. The first position got a certificate and a 10000 naira cash prize. The three-week orientation wound down with glitz and funfair with the youths refreshed and obviously invigorated for the task ahead.

The inauguration ceremony finally took place on March 5, 2011. Venue was the NYSC camp, Ede. The ceremony was conceived and executed as a landmark event. Dignitaries who attended it included all the major royal fathers in the state of Osun, all major political figures, representatives of governors of neighbouring ACN states, etc. The governor himself, all members of his cabinet and all members of OYES implementation committee were all dressed in OYES fatigue. The event was covered live by all local and satellite television stations and streamed live on the internet. Its climax was that point when the commandante presented the 20,000 cadet volunteers to the governor. Having received them, the latter, Rauf Aregbesola gave approval for their deployments to different places of primary assignment.

CHAPTER FOUR

DEPLOYMENT AND EXIT PROGRAMME

When a nation exalts Philosophy because it is a noble profession, and debases Plumbing because it is a humble occupation, neither its theories, nor its pipes, will hold water.

Professor Babatunde Fafunwa

I

In chapter two, it was pointed out that quite a number of the candidates who enlisted with OYES were highly qualified. Some had undertaken higher diploma programmes in polytechnics and completed degree programmes in Universities, coming out at the end with good grades. Some even paraded postgraduate qualifications. A handful of them were really well endowed. And their hopes had been that as soon as they had graduated and undergone the mandatory one-year youth corps service, they would settle down to fulfilling careers in any of the major sectors or industries including oil, banking, communications, aviation, construction, power, civil/public service, etc. As it has turned out for them however, several years after receiving the NYSC discharge certificates, their original hopes were beginning to look like mirages. They continued to walk the streets, hoping against forlorn hopes for some kind of miracle that would transform their original dreams into reality.

In initiating OYES therefore, and beyond the temporary two-year reprieve that it offered them, the plan was to capture most of these young men and women, give them a new orientation and get them to understand and accept life's concrete realities, as unfortunate as they might now appeared to be. It also entailed introducing them to alternative ways of confronting these realities, no matter how modest these might be.

The alternatives, directly, consisted of getting them to take fresh looks at those professions and vocations which, as idealistic young men and women they had always regarded with attitudes of condescension, or even thought of as completely demeaning. These vocations could, in truth, be humble and would include such ones as plumbing, baking, farming, bead making, fashion designing, photography, automobile repairs, poultry keeping and others similar to them. But in getting the volunteers to re-examine their attitudes toward them, the aim was to make them find out if any of them suited their talents, if there were some of them they could variously exploit as means of sustenance and, even, sources of fulfilment after they might have concluded their OYES programme.

The process of achieving this could never have been easy. Every young person has his/her own sense of pride. Legitimately so - and the fact that he/she had not been able to start a career several years after leaving school would, in most probability, be causing him/her some feeling of humiliation already. Asking such people to dismount completely from their horses of self pride, no matter how weak in strength the animals might now have become, could be considered as akin to rubbing salt into their wounds. But realizing this on the part of the managers of OYES did not mean they had to abandon the idea. After all, the key word in the name of the scheme is "empowerment", and NOT "employment", and the project would not have achieved this objective – of empowerment - if, at the end of two years, the volunteers had gained nothing else beyond the sum of two hundred and forty thousand naira which, individually, their monthly stipend totalled up to, if they simply returned to the streets without having acquired any skills, if they had not learned to believe in themselves, or cultivated an attitude of self dependence.

Public Works Green Gang Sheriff Corps Traffic Marshall Osun Paramedics Sanitation Czars

So, as the programme was conceptualized, the process of re-orientation was to commence during the three-week training period. And if we go back to chapter three and take another look at the analysis of the series of lessons delivered during the theoretical part of the programme, it will be discovered that they were geared toward making the trainees take another look at themselves, the outlook they had hitherto held toward life, and thereafter adopt a fresh perspective and prepare themselves for new challenges. Indeed, the epigraph with which this chapter has been prefaced is a quoted statement of late Aliu

Babatunde Fafunwa, Professor of Education and former Federal Minister of Education. It was taken from "OYES: Know Yourself and Why You Are Here", a lecture delivered by Engineer Daniyan during the training of the first batch of OYES in 2011. The aim of this particular lesson, as its title suggests, was to make participant trainees undergo a process of individual self re-examination. In a sub-section of the lesson, the trainees were told pointedly that the reason why they had decided to enlist on the programme was because they had chosen individually to "develop a vocational career as a secure route to a brighter future," and that "to succeed, what you need is not simply improving on the way you do things. You need a total overhaul of your habits and how you see life." The lecturer made the point of adding the quotation from Fafunwa in order to force an appreciation of the dialectics of life on the participant trainees. The so-called noble professions that are exalted cannot be of any impact if a society fails to accord due respect to those trained in the "humble" ones. A philosopher will not be able to devote required attention to his/her work if he/she has no water to bathe with, cook food with, or carry out his/her laundry. In other words, he/she would need the services of a plumber who possesses the competence to fix pipes and ensure that the taps in the philosopher's residence are running before the latter could have the comfort of thinking through, and eventually committing into writing, the novel ideas that he has just discovered. Implication: a society needs a plumber as much as it does a philosopher.

The lessons regarding the inter-dependence of people and professions instilled in the cadets during the training were to be transformed into practice during the period of their deployment. It was indeed a deliberate policy of OYES implementation committee to deploy volunteers – all of them – into either of two general areas for the first three months immediately after training. The two areas are street clearing and weeding of road verges. Here is how the commandante puts it during the interview: "So, for the first three months, whoever you are in OYES, you will do one of those two, or, in fact, both: sweeping the streets and clearing the weed on road verges."

In addition to the goal of instilling an attitude of re-orientation in the cadets, another reason for deploying the cadets to sanitation and public works had to do with the fact that when Aregbesola and his team first came into office, cleaning Osun towns and cities of filth represented one of the most urgent tasks confronting the new government. For, as Kola Omotunde-Young revealed in a discussion with this writer, the new administration arrived to find that roads and highways in the state were literally overflowing with garbage and wastes. As he added, "no one was removing garbage from the streets the way it is done every day now and taken for granted, (and, as a consequence), the drainages were blocked and dirty and rain water just flowed unto the roads. "Determined to rescue the streets and clean the state of filth, the new government found a ready workforce in the army of OYES volunteers it had just recruited

But as the commandante made clear in an interview I had with him, a few of the volunteers in the 2011 batch were taken aback when it was repeated to them that they would have to sweep streets or weed grasses on road verges. Repeated is the word, really, because, the information had already been conveyed to them in the various forms of advertisement sent out, calling for applications. As it would seem though, picking the information from the news or reading it in fliers and handbills was not the same thing as being confronted with the reality of it. This seems to be the only way to explain the reluctance on the part of a few of the volunteers to subject themselves to cleaning streets and clearing drainages; and why a few of them, especially those with postgraduate degrees, decided in the end to excuse themselves from the programme. It bears repeating that the number was negligible, as most of the others decided to swallow their prides and adjust.

Following the three-month period of compulsory sanitation and public works, a cadet would then be deployed into any of the seven areas of focus of OYES. These areas have been listed out in chapter two but will still be discussed in relatively more details now.

Cleaning major streets and weeding of grass on road verges still remains number one. Those deployed to do this were known as **sanitation czars**.

Idowu Adedeji was one of such cadets. She is from Osogbo Local Government and participated as a pioneer volunteer in the 2011-2013 batch. She confirmed in an interview that the primary assignment given to sanitation czars was to "clean up Osun" and make sure that all major streets in all major towns and cities in the state were sparklingly clean latest by seven o'clock every morning. When asked how she felt when she was first told that her major assignment would be to sweep major streets, her answer in effect confirmed what commandante had earlier given as the typical reactions of most of the cadets. Here is Mrs Adedeji, as she spoke in Yoruba:

> A koko ro pe egbe titi bawo! Sugbon nigba ti a de ibe, a ri wipe awon kan ma wa ti won fe ma gba ile yi gan, bi o tie je pe 5000 naira ni awon o ma gba gan. Ti o je wipe ki anfani yi tie yo fun won, ni awa wa ri ni ofe lofo, bi gbogbo wa se be mo niyen la ba bere si ni je anfani yen lo diedie.
>
> TRANSLATION
>
> Initially we didn't feel good about it, but when we got there, we realized that there were a lot of people out there who desired the opportunity to do such work even at a monthly pay of 5,000 naira, but could not get it. With that thought, we saw it as an opportunity and we embraced it. (My translation)

The second major area of deployment was in maintenance of public infrastructure. Those deployed here were known as **public works brigades**. Here, volunteers who possessed technical competence in certain areas were deployed to rehabilitate, repair, maintain and renovate infrastructural facilities belonging to the state. These included roads, school and hospital buildings, electrical fittings, water pipelines and roads drainages. Such volunteers worked under the supervision of relevant experts in the state Ministry of Works including engineers, architects and quantity surveyors. Other cadets deployed as public works brigades were charged with clearing of refuse and debris from gutters, walkways and highways. Fortunately, the new government met some newly purchased garbage trucks when it came into office. The trucks had not been used at all and were already beginning to develop faults. As was also discovered, they were really not of good quality and, additionally, adequate arrangement was not made for their repairs and maintenance. Not ready to allow them go to rot, the new administration did all it could to deploy them for use and keep them working. They were made available to all local governments and it was these trucks that were now used to dispose whatever wastes and refuse that were collected from the streets.

The third group was known as **sheriff corps**. Members of sheriff corps functioned, more or less, as state police charged, as they were, with maintaining security. They were first made to undergo some training in security maintenance. Simbiat Ajibike Ilyasu who worked as a sheriff corps member in the 2013-2015 batch described the training in an interview with this writer as intensive, its only limit being that it did not include how to carry gun. As she further stated, the training first started in Ilesha and was later continued at NYSC camp, Ede. She added that, the sessions were "coordinated by soldiers who lectured and gave us instructional materials." The final part of it as she further stated took place in the Government House. It was a parade in which soldiers and mobile policemen took part and which the governor himself attended.

Following the training, a sheriff corps member would then be posted to one out of three units. The first unit was involved in neighbourhood security. Cadets in this category were charged with preventing petty crimes. The second unit was known as GMT, short form for Governor's Monitoring Team. Cadets deployed were placed under the charge of the police commander of the governor's formal security outfit and they followed the governor wherever he went within the state functioning as part of his protocol team and assisting mainly in the area of crowd control. The third unit represented, originally, the nucleus of the Swift Action Squad (SAS) set up by the state government in 2012. Simbiat Ilyasu revealed that she originally worked under the Swift

Action Squad, adding that part of their duties at the time included arresting those involved in illegal gold mining in Ilesha area and handing them over to the police. She went on to add that, another aspect of their duties, which was actually similar to the first one, was monitoring those who engaged in illegal logging, apprehending them and, again, handing them over to the formal police.

The fourth group was known as **green gang**. Those in this category were simply involved in the preservation of environments and beautification of cities and towns. They created parks and gardens and, as well planted trees and flowers along major streets and routes within and between cities and towns in the state.

Cadets in the fifth group were known as **traffic marshals**. These worked as traffic wardens, controlling traffic in cities and towns and assisting in reducing, even checking, violations of traffic jams and congestions. Working in conjunction with the state Ministry of Works and Transport, traffic managers also helped generate revenues for the state through fines imposed on drivers who violated traffic regulations. Mrs Toyin Adeleke was one such cadet who served as traffic manager. Adeleke narrated her experience as a traffic marshal in an interview with one of my research assistants, Sade Adewale - Lawal.

As she said, they were initially made to undergo a two-week training programme in traffic control when they first reported for duty at the state Ministry of Works and Transport. At the end of the training, as she continued, they were posted to different points in different parts of the state to control traffic. What many of her colleagues at the time found objectionable with the posting was the fact that they had to report at their post every morning at 7 o'clock, and close at 4 o'clock in the afternoon. On this, they demanded to know if they would receive any extra allowance for having to close much later than the rest of their colleagues. Many left on being told that they were not entitled to anything of such. Adeleke said that she, on her own part, decided to stay back and that, going over the decision afterwards, she felt happy that she decided against rejecting the posting. It is important to listen to her as she spoke directly with Sade Adewale - Lawal:

> When we got to OYES traffic marshal, we were many, we were up to 70 cadets that were deployed to Traffic marshal. Lot of them then was asking if their salary would be increased for closing as late as four o'clock. They told them the salary would not be increased. We were collecting 10,000 naira at the initial stage. When we got to traffic marshal, some said they could not cope with the situation; not closing till 4pm on a 10,000 naira salary. So they went away. With all these, I endured. I was closing by 4pm and receiving 10,000 naira

> at the end of the month. Later our salary was increased to 15,000 naira and we were afterwards given permanent appointments.

The sixth group was known as **paramedics**. Those deployed here were those who had formal training as health superintendents, nurses and even drivers. They worked with the O'Ambulance Scheme and were found on the highways, driving around in well-equipped ambulances. Their tasks were to offer assistance in emergency situations, perform rescue operations in cases of accidents, render first aids to victims and promptly take them to nearby hospitals.

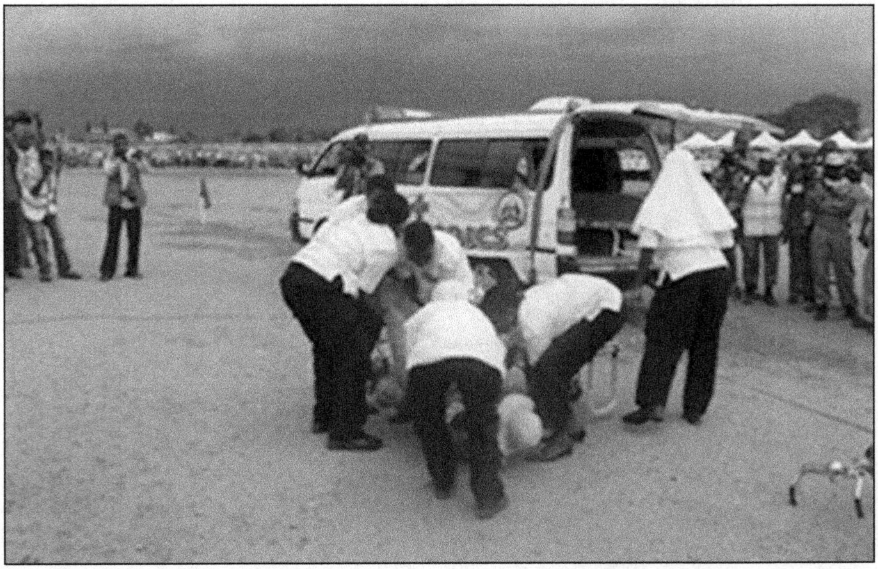

Mudasiru Ojekale is one such cadet posted to O'Ambulance. He is from Egbedore Local Government with headquarters in Awo. He was a driver and served with O'Ambulance for three years beginning from 2014. Ojekale explained his job description to Sade Adewale Lawal in an interview. He spoke in Yoruba but an English translation is provided immediately after the Yoruba original.

> O ni unit kookan ti won ti allocate awon motor kookan si. Bi iru emi nisinyi, mo wa ni under Awo Local Government. Highway to wa ni under Awo Local Government. So, any emergency to ba sele ni gbogbo ibeyen titi ti a fi maa de Iwo,

> awa la ma cover e - starting from Dele Yes Sir Roundabout de Iwo, awa la ma cover e de Awo.
>
> The ambulances have been allocated to specific routes. For instance, I work in Awo Local Government. Any incidence from that point to Iwo, we respond to it. My route extends from Dele Yes Sir Roundabout to Iwo. (My translation)

The last group is the **teachers' corps**. Volunteers in this category are those who possessed teaching qualifications like TC II, NCE and B.ED/B.A (Ed.)/B.Sc (Ed.). They were deployed to public primary and secondary schools which had shortages of teachers. The State Universal Basic Education Board (SUBEB) was charged with the responsibility of screening those to be deployed to primary schools while the Post Primary Schools Teaching Service Commission (TESCOM) had the task of screening those to be posted to secondary schools.

Rukayat Adeola Fabunmi represents an example of such volunteers who were deployed to teach in Osun public schools. Fabunmi enlisted as a volunteer in the 2013-2015 batch. She is from Osogbo Local Government and held an NCE of the Osun State College of Education, Ilesa. In an interview with Adetokunbo Shittu, Fabunmi confirmed that a cadet had to possess requisite teaching qualifications before he/she could be deployed under the teachers' corps. In addition to this, he/she also had to sit for an examination, the purpose of which was to ensure that the cadet in question actually earned the qualification being brandished. Though her period of cadetship ended in 2015, Adeola Fabunmi continued to teach under SUBEB for much long after. The ten thousand naira she received monthly as an OYES volunteer, and the additional five thousand naira she was paid as a member of the teachers' corps represents her only source of income.

* * * * *

As can be seen, the services rendered by OYES cadets covered a wide gamut of areas. In other words, the relationship that existed between them and the state can be considered as symbiotic. While government offered them fresh hopes, provided them with means of sustenance and gave them opportunities of a fresh start, they too contributed in no small measure to the progress of the state. This precisely was in tune with the vision and mission that propelled the setting up of the scheme in the first place.

Originally, the plan was to provide distinct uniforms for each of the seven identified areas but funding problems forced the implementation committee to modify this somewhat. All the same, each of traffic marshals, sheriff corps and paramedics still got uniforms which served the purpose of distinguishing each one of them, first from the other, and, then from the rest of the volunteers.

Since OYES volunteers were deployed at the local government levels, there were officers appointed to monitor their activities at this level. The officer charged with the overall supervision of all the cadets in a local government was known as a **mentor**. The post of mentor was reserved exclusively for retired police or military officers. Working directly under a mentor were the **prefects, deputy prefects** and **provosts.** Usually these three were chosen from among the volunteers. Before any volunteers could however be so appointed, he/she would have been under observation for a while and certified to possess the requisite qualities of leaders which included charisma, integrity, honesty and sense of responsibility. Mudashiru Ojekale who worked as a prefect in Egbedore Local Government in the 2011-2013 batch said his duty at the time included assigning cadets posted under him to units on a daily basis and ensuring that each of such cadets had portions to work on. The duty of ensuring that every cadet in each unit worked duly on his/her portion rested in a leader who was charged with the direct coordination of the unit. So at the end of each day, the leader would file a report on the activities and behaviour of cadets assigned to him/her to the prefect, deputy prefect or provost, as the case might be, and he/she would in turn submit a report on the activities carried out in the units under his supervision to the mentor. The mentor reported to the OYES head office in Osogbo. The final responsibility of certifying that a cadet had in any particular month discharged his/her duty and therefore deserved to receive his/her stipend was vested in the commandante. Any cadet who consistently defaulted in his/her duty without being able to provide satisfactory explanations for it, or otherwise indulged in behaviour considered to be against the objective of the scheme was expected to be summarily delisted. Conversely, and since it was a volunteer scheme, any cadet who wished to disengage from the scheme was expected to submit a written notice of his intention to the commandante. Once this was done, he/she would be discharged immediately.

Finally, there was also a provision for what was called **collaboration** in the scheme. This referred to a situation where an individual, organization, agency or a department, parastatal or ministry of a state or federal government felt that in the course of executing a project, he/she/it required the assistance or expertise of any group of OYES volunteers. In such a situation, all that needed to be done was for the individual(s) or group that was in need of such services to write a formal application to the management of OYES, explaining the project and, as well, area(s) of need. On receiving such application, OYES would conduct some investigation to ascertain the authenticity of the project and its relevance to the focus of the scheme. Once the report of the investigation came out positive, the number of cadets which had been requested for would be released to the individual or organization that made the request. Iskilu Bolarinwa, a pioneer cadet from Osogbo Local Government gave examples of collaborative engagements that he had been part of in an interview with Adetokunbo Shittu, one of my research assistants:

> **Shittu**: How does collaboration which you just talked about work?
>
> **Bolarinwa**: It is those organisations that got impressed by our works in the communities that collaborated with OYES. Ministries and Organisations asked for our services. Each time they came, we obliged them and went with other junior cadet members to do the work assigned.
>
> **Shittu**: Thank you very much. Can you mention some of the beneficial programmes to which the OYES cadets were invited?

Bolarinwa: I remember vividly our work with the water corporation. OWMA too collaborated with us by assigning us some duties. We also did some work for the Ministry of Education when they were about to start the school feeding programme.

Shittu: OMEAL?

Bolarinwa: OMEAL. Then we did a research to find out how many pupils were in each class from primary 1-3

Shittu: So, it was the OYES cadets that researched to provide statistical data on the population of pupils in the schools?

Bolarinwa: Yes, in each primary school. Government acted based on the outcome of our research. They could tell precisely the number of students being prepared for in each school.

It is probably necessary to shed more light on the project that Iskilu Bolarinwa was referring to here. What happened, precisely, was that when the state government wanted to introduce the school feeding programme, the Ministry of Education together with the State Universal Basic Education Board (SUBEB) was asked to provide information on total enrolment of pupils in the state primary, middle and high schools. The Ministry turned in a figure of about 750,000. The Governor, thinking of the need to verify it had then directed that OYES cadets be deployed for that purpose. The verification exercise showed that there actually were slightly less than 450,000 pupils in the three levels in the state. Government was thus able to save a considerable amount of money as a consequence of the exercise.

But the purpose of introducing the bit on collaboration into the scheme was to give cadets the opportunity of gaining exposure, acquiring new experiences thus increasing their chances of securing lasting employment at the end of the two-year period of engagement. As explained by the commandante, collaboration was a voluntary aspect of the scheme and, indeed, a volunteer had the choice of refusing to join a collaborative project. As he says: "If a person refuses and says, I don't want to participate in that collaboration, I won't fight you. But the only thing is that I will throw you out if I say sweep, or do this work and you don't do it..."

But there was another dimension to the issue of collaboration in OYES. Indeed, following the crash training programme they were made to undergo, OYES cadets were also seen as additional manpower that could be deployed by different agencies of government as they pursued their primary objectives. Because of this, the group of cadets in each of the already identified areas of postings operate in collaboration with relevant agencies of government. Directly, O-Ambulance operated in collaboration with the state Ministry of Health, Public Works and Traffic Marshalls worked in collaboration with the Ministry of Works, Green Gang was in affiliation with the Ministry of Environment, Teachers Corps as earlier indicated was under the State Universal Basic Education Board while the Sanitation Gang collaborated with the Osun Waste Management Agency (OWMA). On its own, Osun Rural Enterprise and Agricultural Programme (OREAP) undertook the training of thousands of OYES cadets who were subsequently deployed into farming, following the expiration of their period of cadetship. What this meant then was that, by conception, OYES represented a complex programme of collaboration with the different arms of the government of the state of Osun.

II

Exit programme is the third part of the two-year scheme – after deployment and collaboration. And, as it must have been made clear in the brief comments with which this chapter was opened, it is that part of the OYES programme that gave meaning to the central word in the name of the scheme – **empowerment**.

Exit programme referred to the training which the cadets were made to undergo; aimed at making them acquire skills that made it possible for them to continue to sustain themselves after their two year period of temporary appointment had lapsed. Jamiu Ibrahim, a former cadet who was later deployed to work as media assistant to OYES commandante described it as some kind of "take home skill" which every cadet needed to keep him/her engaged long after he/she must have graduated from OYES. On his own, Iskilu Bolarinwa saw it as a form of training in "self-reliance and competence." Both cadets put the issue well. In a time of profound economic crisis, not many people could secure positions in white collar establishments. People therefore needed to learn to look inwards, examine themselves and see what innate talents and abilities of theirs could be developed and put to use in their struggles to earn a living. In other words, teaching cadets to be self-dependent served as the goal of the exit package incorporated into OYES programme.

The details of the exit programme evolved over a considerable period of time. There were, in the end, quite many of them but, together, they could be classified under five broad but complexly inter-related fields. They were: 1) Agriculture, 2) Trades and Craftsmanship, 3) Home Economics, 4) Information and Communication Technology (ICT) and 5), Sponsorship to Foreign Countries.

Agriculture and its multi-dimensional forms enjoyed, by far, the greatest encouragement of the different forms of exit programmes promoted by OYES. For cadets who demonstrated interest in the field, opportunities for specialization covered almost the entire gamut of its complex value chain. For crop production, areas in which cadets were provided with training sponsorship included cultivation, harvesting and marketing of products. And this also involved different kinds of crops, using innovative methods. In the interview conducted with him that I have continued to refer to, the commandante informed our research team of the establishment of OYES Farmers' Brigade in all the thirty Local Government areas and Ife East Area Authority. The Brigade, as he further revealed in the interview, specialized in the production of Orange Fleshed Sweet Potato (OFSP), describing it as "a hybrid formulated sweet potato that is vitamin A laden." And vitamin A, as is well known is good for the eye, and also for the brain. The product, as Col. Oyewole (rtd) further made clear, was being sold to O'Meal which was at the time "using it to feed our children and we are getting the money to rotate again to OYES."

Yet another area in which OYES provided training for its cadets was mechanised tomato and cucumber production. This was executed in collaboration with Fidelity Enterprises located in Mosan – Ijebu in Ogun State. Fidelity supplied its products to Shoprite supermarkets in Lagos and Ibadan. The commandante revealed that eleven OYES cadets were as at the time when the interview was being conducted with him receiving training in the company.

A significant number of cadets were also exposed to different aspects of animal science, including poultry keeping, dairy production and processing, fisheries, egg production, meat processing, piggery, etc. In this regard, and especially for some of the highly technical areas, OYES had to enter into collaboration with institutions which had expertise in them. Colonel Oyewole (rtd) specifically cited as an example, the Faculty of Agriculture of Obafemi Awolowo University which, he said, assisted in providing training to cadets in ram fattening and how to raise turkey.

Trades and craftsmanship was the second major field of emphasis in the exit programme. Here, in fact, hundreds of OYES volunteers received free training in a wide gamut of vocations including auto repairs, welding, electrical fittings, plumbing, photography, painting and decoration, carpentry and joinery, air conditioning and refrigerating and tiling. Having acquired competence in one or the other of these trades and, following the expiration of their period of cadetship, several of them went ahead to set up shops for themselves.

A slightly different dimension of this case of empowerment of cadets in trades and craftsmanship is best illustrated with the case of Jamiu Ibrahim, a former OYES volunteer who, as stated earlier, secured a permanent employment as media assistant to the commandante. At the end of his secondary school education, Jamiu, due to one reason or the other, could not continue his formal education. Instead, what he did was to enrol as an apprentice in photography. Jamiu did this for three years, beginning from 2006, and by 2009, was due for graduation. Unfortunately however, he could not raise the money to buy a professional camera which was a critical requirement for graduation. Due to this reality, Jamiu literally remained in limbo. Then came the opportunity of OYES and the young man applied. The application was successful, and he became an OYES cadet. It is probably better to hear the rest of the story directly from him as he presented it to Sade Adewale Lawal in an interview:

> **Adewale - Lawal**: You said you told your daddy that you wanted to learn photography, and you also said that it was when you got to OYES that you did your ND in Mass Communication and specialized in photography, does it mean you have been learning about it before coming to OYES?
>
> **Jamiu**: Yes. OYES empowers me in photography. I have been learning it, but I could not afford to buy the equipment
>
> **Adewale - Lawal**: But you said you were working with the daily post?
>
> **Jamiu**: No, I was just the graphics editor
>
> **Sade**: Before you got to OYES?
>
> **Jamiu**: Yes. That was 2010 to 2011. I have learnt it (photography) between 2006 and 2009. I learnt photography and graphic design. So when I got appointment with daily post, I specialized in editing and packaging of the page. When I got to OYES, the first camera I bought, I borrowed 8,000 naira to buy the trash camera. So I later realized 58,000 naira from OYES to buy a digital camera which I used for my freedom in photography. I learnt it, but (was) unable to do the freedom. It was when I got to OYES that I realized the money that I used to buy a professional camera needed for my freedom.

It is necessary to complete Jamiu Ibrahim's story before moving on. As can be gleaned from the chat he had with Sade Adewale Lawal, Jamiu would no longer be content with becoming a professional photographer.

Rather, he enlisted for an ND programme in Mass Communication at the Osun State Polytechnic, Ire. He was able to pay his fees from the savings he made from the stipend he received monthly as an OYES cadet and the photography he practised by the side. The rest of the story – which is that he now has a permanent appointment with OYES - is already known to us.

The third area of emphasis in exit programme has been broadly described as Home Economics. This was equally wide and it generally involved making things needed for general domestic use like liquid soap, balm, cream, different kinds of disinfectants, face powder and such things that form part of make-up kits. Quite a number of cadets also specialized in baking – cakes, in the main – and, as well, events planning and decoration. Idowu Adedeji whose name I cited earlier on in this chapter also represents one good example of former cadets who benefitted in this area of exit training. She learned to make liquid soap and disinfectant while still a cadet and this, as she told Sade Adewale - Lawal in an interview is what she had to depend on for sustenance after the expiration of her period of stay in OYES. The relevant aspect of the interview is reproduced below. Adedeji spoke in Yoruba but an English translation of the interview is provided immediately after the Yoruba original below.

> **Adedeji**: … Nigba ti a bere si ni je anfani e, a mo wipe nkankan tun wa labe ile gbigba yi ti o ju ile gbigba yi lo. Lara awon nkan ti o wa labe pe a gba ile yii nipe, won introduce awon programme kookan ti a pe ni exit programme si wa nigba yen. Lara awon exit programme yen ni O'Reap wa, lara e ni Odua Farm Settlement wa. Lara e ni won ti ko wa ni liquid soap ati disinfectant ti emi nje anfani e loni, ti mo fi nse ise se lowolowo bayi
>
> **Sade**: E ko mo nipa e rara tele, ki won to ko yin?
>
> **Adedeji**: Mi o mo nipa e rara tele. Ninu OYES ni mo ti ko. Ohun ni mo de nfi se ise se loni, ti mo joko ti, ti mo nje loni. Mi o ni ise mi leyin re ti mo nje. Liquid wash yen ati disinfectant ohun ni mon se. die lara awon liquid wash yen, being pe mo fe travel, mi o ni production nile bayi, sugbon mo ni liquid wash nile, mo de ni awon disinfectant ti mi o ti ro. O si wa ninu jerry can. Then lara awon disinfectant yen, awon kan wa ni OYES office to je wipe ti e ba de ibe e ma ri

OYES disinfectant ni ara re, ti o je wipe emi ni mo se. ti o de je wipe won nta nibe. Nibeyen, mo tun nri owo. OYES office gangan ni white house, o wa nibe lowolowo bi mo se nsoro yi. Phone number mi wa lara e. Emi ti mo se naa niyi

Sade: Se OYES office ti ibi ti awon eeyan ma npe ni Aregbesola?

Adedeji: Beeni, ibe lo wa. So, t'eyan ba de ibe, e o ba nibe. Mo de tun nko awon eeyan bi won se nse liquid wash yen, sugbon emi o ni ibi kankan ti mo ti ko. Inu OYES yen ni mo ti je anfani yen. Ti o je wipe kii se pe won ni kin mu owo wa ki nwa fi ko tabi kin mu obi wa. Nigba yen lohun ti won ni ki a wa ko, won mu eeyan mejimeji ni local government kookan. A de ni 31 local governments ni Osun state nigbayen. Thirty one local governments yen, won mu eeyan mejimeji. Mo je okan lara awon eeyan meji ti won mu ni Osogbo local government nigbayen. So, lara awon ti won mu nigbayen ti won ni ki a wa se oriire, ki won wa je anfani ekose yen, emi je enikan ti mo nfi se ise se lowolowo bayi, ti mo fi njeun loni, to je wipe mi o ni nkan miran pelu e.

TRANSLATION

Adedeji: When we started the work, we never knew there were some other hidden benefits. Part of the hidden benefit is the exit programme which was later introduced to us. The exit programme includes, O'Reap, Odua Farm Settlement, and training on how to make liquid soap and disinfectant which I do today as a source of livelihood...

Adewale - Lawal: You knew nothing about it before you were taught?

Adedeji: I knew nothing about it before then. I learnt about it from OYES, and that is what I have as my sole source of sustenance today. I have just a little production on ground now, because I am travelling. If not, I normally produce it in large quantity. The disinfectant I produce, labelled "OYES disinfectant" is sold at OYES office. That gives me additional money. My phone number is on the label which indicates that I produce it. It is presently at the white house.

Adewale - Lawal: Do you mean the OYES office located in the area generally referred to as Aregbesola?

Adedeji: Yes. That is where my disinfectant is being sold. I also train people on how to produce the liquid soap. I never had any knowledge of it before. I learnt it from OYES without paying anything for the training. When the training was introduced to us, two people were chosen from each local government, and we had thirty-one local governments in Osun state then. I was one of the two people chosen from Osogbo local government. So, out of all of us chosen for the training then, I am one of those who live by what I have made of the training today. I do not have any other source of income apart from this.

Later on in the interview, Adedeji added that beside liquid soap and disinfectants, some other cadets trained in how to make air freshener and bleach. She stated that on the day of the passing out parade, many of them displayed some of the things they had learned to make and that the governor in fact bought some of them, distributing them to some of the monarchs who were present at the event that day.

A second story was narrated by Jamiu Ibrahim. It was that of a female volunteer who, according to him, trained in how to use Ankara wax to make hand bags and shoes. He gave the woman's name as Olaosebikan, stating that she was from Ife East local government. She was specifically sent to Lagos for the training, and she returned perfectly competent in her area of specialization. As Jamiu said, she could "even use Ankara to make bouquet used by brides in weddings."

Information and Communication Technology (ICT) was the fourth area of training for which OYES cadets were sponsored. Opportunities available here could actually be described as fantastic as they include both local and overseas training sponsorship. With regards to local training, RLG Nigeria served as the steering partner of the Osun Youth Empowerment Scheme. Starting from 2011 when the programme was inaugurated, not less than five thousand (5000) cadets received training in their centre located in Ilesa. The training, as Seye Adeoti put it in a short report published in Volume 1, No 1, of *Apalara*, the official OYES magazine, "is geared towards providing youths in the State of Osun with a deep and broad knowledge of the theoretical framework in ICT and the application of those theories in the maintenance and assembling of mobile phones, Computers, etc" (p. 6). As for overseas training, hundreds of volunteers were sent out to countries like India, Pakistan and Ghana to acquire competence in ICT. On their return, a number of them were assisted to secure employment in Adulawo Technology Centre, the technical workshop of RLG which was also established in Ilesa. In fact, as the commandante revealed, the establishment of that centre was predicated on the condition that it would give preference to OYES graduates in ICT when it came to matters of employment. He further added, the commandante that is, that in fact, eighty five percent of those who currently work at the centre were former OYES volunteers.

Sponsorship to foreign countries which I have listed as the fifth form of exit training would seem to be repeating the one just discussed above. Well, an important additional point to make here is that there were no restrictions with regards to the purpose for which a cadet was sent abroad. ICT is important, no doubt, but several other volunteers were sent to foreign countries to receive training in other fields. For example, most of the cadets that travelled to Germany went there for the purpose of exposure to mechanized Agriculture. With regards to those who went to Cuba, the primary reason was to learn lessons in how to be self-dependent. Iskilu Bolarinwa, a former cadet from Osogbo Local Government was one of the beneficiaries of sponsored trips to the small island country located off the coast of Florida. He gave a report of his experience to Adetokunbo Shittu in an interview. He too spoke in Yoruba but, as usual, an English translation of his testimony is provided immediately after the Yoruba original.

> **Shittu**: A gbo pe ijoba ipinle osun ran awon agunbaniro OYES kan lo si Cuba, e de ni anfani ati oore ofe lati lo pelu won. S e le so die fun wa nipa e?
>
> **Bolarinwa**: Lori oro Cuba, surprise lo je fun mi because… less than a week ni mo sese mo pe Cuba la fe lo. Won kan pe mi, 'se o ni nkan bayi, boya national ID card?' mo ni mii ni. 'ki lo ni?' mo ni international passport. 'okay, fine, lo mu wa.' Mo de submit e sibe lai mo nkan ti won fe fi se. the first month, second month, third month. Moni, 'ah, e kan gba passport mi, e o so anything fun mi. e ba mi mu passport mi.' won ni k'emi ma lo jare. Igba to de ya to ku less than a month ti a maa travel, won de pe wa pe… ki a se awon documentation kan. A sa se awon documentation. After that…boya bi three days or four days mo de receive call pe we are to report at Ola Oni Centre for moving to Cuba. I was surprised. Won honour mi. A de take off…a lo. A de Cuba…Cuba is good, mi o ti experience pe an travel ri. Bo ti e sepe a ti n try pe a fe travel tele ti Olorun o tii kadara, but igba ti state government de recognize wa ti Olorun de sope tiwon la maa ba lo. We were five in number ti a lo lati ipase OYES from different Local Governments. I am from Osogbo, we have Rafiu from Ila, we have Seun from Ede, one particular guy from Iwo and a particular guy from Ife. Cuba experience, life won so simple… although won ni challenges to sepe challenges won…style of living won yato si tiwa nibibayi. They have a problem with the US. US o je ki country kankan o partner pelu won therefore gbogbo nkan ti won lo is what they have been using for long. Won ni maintenance culture gidi gan. They are into farming. Farming won at least a particular person to ba ni farm land o le ni less than minimum of 2 acres of land. And each farm land has its own tractor. Ko de si bo se le wu ki tractor na old to, o si ma ma sise. Which means won ni maintenance culture. Ko dabi tiwa nibi bayi to se pe we Nigerians a o ni maintenance culture. It is one of the

experiences ti a ni. then ninu research wa, a tun se research debi wipe the union leaders, bi won se je union yen won tun ni farm land: hectares of farm lands ni each province ti won de gba workers sibe. At the end of the day ti won ba harvest ti won ba ta ni international market gain ti won ba ri nibe, won a divide e into three: won de ma ko percentage kan fun government, awon na ma share percentage kan and the other third one won ma share fun awon workers. Ko le sele ni Nigeria. Boya ile ti o maa mo lola o, Olorun le se ko ribe. And they don't believe in government must do everything for us. Government support won. You cannot go to Cuba pe mo kan fe lo stay tori challenges ti won ni…won believe in their own production. They believe in handy work. Won believe npe nkan ti a ba se la ma je ninu e. aso ti a se la n wo. Won o ko aso wa lati foreign country kankan.

TRANSLATION

Shittu: We learnt that the state government took some cadet members to Cuba, and you happened to be one of them. Can you tell us a little about that?

Bolarinwa: On the Cuba issue: it was a total surprise for me because, I had no idea I would be going there until about a week to departure. I was called and asked if I had a national ID card. I said no. I was asked further if I had an international passport and I said yes. I was asked to submit it without being informed of the reason why. I complied, but after a few months and there was no news as to why I was asked to submit the document, I got curious and went to ask what was happening and to see if I could retrieve my passport, but I was sent back. However, when it was about a month to the trip, we were invited to process some documents. About three days later, I received a call to report at Ola Oni Centre, from where we were to depart for Cuba. I was surprised and felt greatly honoured. Cuba is good. I had never travelled outside the country before then; though I have made efforts in the past but it seemed God had destined it that it was through OYES that the dream would come to pass. We were five cadets in all chosen from different Local Governments. We were five in all. I am

> from Osogbo Local Government; we have Rafiu from Ila, Seun from Ede, a guy from Iwo and another from Ife. The Cubans live a very simple life style. They have challenges which make their way of life different from ours. They have problem with the US and the US has prohibited other countries from assisting them. Therefore, they rely on old but functional technologies. They have high maintenance culture. They survive on farming and each farmer has at least two acres of land. Each farm land has a tractor which is always in a working condition no matter how old it is. That is an indication of a strong maintenance culture which is lacking here in Nigeria. It is one fascinating experience that I had during the trip. In our research, we also discovered that the union leaders practice agriculture in spite of their being unionists. They have farm lands: hectares of farm lands in each province, worked on by paid employees. At the end of each harvest, the produce is sold at the international market and the proceed is divided into three with a percentage going to government, another to the coffers of the union leaders to be shared as appropriate while the third is used for the payment of workers. That is a feat that a country like Nigeria should look forward to achieving in future. The Cubans also don't believe in waiting on government to get things done for them; however government is trying its best. One cannot go to Cuba with a view to settling down there because of their problems but they believe in what they produce. They pay much premium to handy works. They believe in surviving on their own terms. They wear only those fabrics made in the country and do not rely on importation.

Iskilu Bolarinwa did not mince words. He made it clear that the purpose of the trip he and other colleagues of his undertook to Cuba was to get exposed to the people's lifestyles, their agricultural system and their manufacturing industry. He said the trip made him see what hard work and determination could do. Having observed firsthand how Cubans survived in the face of serious challenges, his imagination became fired. He said he took a decision to venture into manufacturing. He started on a small scale, making laundry soap, bar soap, as well as body and hair cream. He was doing quite well and was right now thinking of setting up his own factory.

III

The focus of this chapter has been on the core of OYES programme. In it, I have devoted time to discussing the twin aspects of deployment and exit programme. I hope that by keeping my discussion of each separate, I have not given the impression that a strict line of demarcation existed between the two. Just in case I have, let me make it clear immediately that both programmes ran concurrently. They impinged on each other. Conceived to run in pari passu, the two together gave meaning to the word "empowerment" which was central to the scheme. A volunteer renders some service to the state in a specific area of deployment. In return for this, he/she was paid a stipend of ten thousand naira. The amount, though small, represented a means of survival, a source of hope. In the course of the two-year period of cadetship, the volunteer was also given an opportunity to learn a specific vocation or, as in the case of Jamiu Ibrahim, complete one that, hitherto, had for one reason or the other, remained in suspension. The skill thus acquired became a means of continued engagement after the affected volunteer must have been discharged from OYES.

It will be correct to cite the cases of cadets who were lucky to be offered permanent appointment in their places of deployment as another instance of empowerment. Clearly, and as many former cadets who now hold such appointments continued to admit, it was OYES that made it possible for them to come across this opportunity in the first instance. Jamiu Ibrahim the current media assistant to OYES commandante is a case in point. Toyin Adeleke who was employed as traffic marshal is another. Both express eternal gratitude to the state government for putting such a scheme in place. Finally, Diran Fashesin, the state coordinator of the scheme, claimed in an interview with this writer that close to five thousand (5000) of those deployed to the teaching service were offered permanent employment in the state teaching service.

This has been a long chapter. Inevitably so, as it has taken on the central aspects of OYES programme. In the course of the discussion, I have, as much as possible, supported the issues raised with testimonies from those who benefitted from either or both sides of the twin programme of deployment and exit programme. Essentially still – in fact wholly – both aspects stood as the direct benefits of the programme. As important as they were, they did not exhaust the whole story. There were those who can be categorized – guardedly – as indirect beneficiaries of the Osun Youth Empowerment Scheme, and it is to them that I will now turn in the next chapter.

CHAPTER FIVE

OYES: INDIRECT BENEFICIARIES

I

In the discussion of the way the Osun Youth Empowerment Scheme (OYES) was designed in chapter two, it was pointed out that the programme was conceived as a kind of para -military agency, in some ways similar to the National Youth Service Corps scheme (NYSC). An important area of difference between the two schemes which ought to be underlined immediately though is that, unlike the latter which is compulsory, OYES is designed to be voluntary. Beyond this, there existed several areas of similarities. One of these lay in the fact that the chief executive of the OYES, just as is the case with NYSC would have to be an individual with a military background, a further implication of the situation being that those enlisted as cadets on the programme would have to wear uniforms, with boots to match.

Coming to agreement on this or what the uniform would look like was not a problem for the implementation committee. Rather, the difficulty that arose lay in the question of how to procure the uniforms, where to get the boots from, how to get the logo and badge, and so on, and so on. In NYSC for example, procurement of uniforms is a big contract, awarded only to big, well known, corporations; and the question this fact confronted the implementation committee with was whether to copy the model.

As Gbenga Odulaja revealed in an interview with this writer, the implementation committee actually contemplated the possibility of awarding the job of designing the uniforms for the first batch of OYES cadets to a contractor from Lagos. The committee earmarked three thousand naira for sewing a set of uniform and, for the first batch, there were forty thousand sets of uniforms in total, since each of the twenty thousand volunteers in that batch was to receive two sets. Altogether then, getting forty thousand uniforms ready for the volunteers in the first batch was to cost the state a total of one hundred and twenty million naira (N120m).

It is a relatively huge sum, indeed an amount which, as Gbenga Odulaja again pointed out during the interview, the implementation committee was reluctant to give out to an individual who was not based in Osun. And that was not all. Because the same kind of question came up when it got to the issue of making boots and shoes for the cadets. And so it did with the badges which were to be affixed to the uniforms. In coming to a decision finally then, the implementation committee reminded itself of the fact that "empowerment" stood as the key word in the OYES project, even if the youths of the state constituted the segment of the population that constituted the target of the empowerment. Since this was the case, the implementation committee thought further, was it not possible to extend the implication of the concept to other disadvantaged segments of the state's population? It answered the question with an affirmative response. And with it began the search for the groups of artisans whose fields of specializations fell within the relevant areas.

II

Alhaji Kola Adegbola, an indigene of Ile Ife, was the national president of the Nigeria Union of Tailors (NUT) between 1994 and 2012. In an interview conducted with him in his shop by this writer on October 28, 2016, Adegbola spoke of how, early in January 2011, a member of his union sent an urgent message to him, asking him to report in Osogbo.

Further information had it that the newly inaugurated government had a job which it wanted to give out to the Nigeria Union of Tailors as a body.

Alhaji Akingbola set out immediately and was on his arrival taken to, as he put it, "one Barrister Gbenga Akano." Barrister Akano asked him if his union was formally registered with the Corporate Affairs Commission and, as well, if it had a Cooperative Society. Alhaji Akingbola's response to the two questions was in the positive and he was asked to produce the certificates of registration of the two organizations. This he did with alacrity. Following this, he and other members of the union together with whom he appeared before the man were directed to the Aregbesola Campaign Office. There, as Akingbola said, they met four or five other officers of the new government who interviewed them. Here is Alhaji Akingbola as he recollected what happened:

> Those we met were about four or five in number. I was there together with my lieutenants. I think we were eleven or so in number the day we met them. They interviewed us and showed us a sample of the OYES uniform which they had sewn in Lagos. They asked us whether, if they gave us the job, we could finish sewing five hundred sets in seventy two hours. We said yes. We negotiated and they told us to come back there again for materials.

Alhaji Akingbola thought quickly. He decided to saddle the responsibility of getting the five hundred sets of uniform ready within the deadline with members of his union who worked and lived within the state capital. The strategy worked and the president and his men returned to the officers who gave them the contract seventy-two hours after with their heads held high. The job was done according to specifications. What followed was totally unexpected: it was a big contract: the Nigeria Union of Tailors would now have to design a total of fifteen thousand sets of uniforms for OYES.

After taking delivery of the fabrics to be used for designing the uniforms, the union called a meeting of the chairpersons of all local government branches in the state including that of Ife East Area office. Here the formula for sharing out the job was worked out. Simply, the decision was that the proportion of the job that would go to each of the local governments would be consistent with the percentage of members in the local government vis-à-vis the total number of registered union members in the state. After this, a deadline which, approximately, translated to one week before the one given by government, was agreed upon. Then the job was shared out, and the mobilisation fee which government had made available, paid. All members followed the instructions given to them by their union. They did a good job and the uniforms were turned in on set deadline. An equivalent number of uniforms was given to the union again for the second batch. The same method was adopted in handling the job and, once more, things worked out extremely well.

As Alhaji Akingbola made it clear during the interview, the development was unprecedented in the history of the union and the excitement it thus generated among members was, again according to him, indescribable. Beyond the personal gains which he admitted members made from the project, the former president laid more emphasis on the positive impact the award of the contract had on his organization. As he stated, before the job came, the faith several members had in the union was already beginning to flag. This was to the extent that when general meetings were called, only about half of the total number of the branches in the state sent representatives. With the winning of the "Aregbe contract" however, members returned en masse to the union. They all now felt very proud to be identified as members of the Nigeria Union of Tailors in Osun State. In an attempt to further strengthen the sense of oneness and unity which now existed among its members, the union decided to set aside a small percentage of the proceeds from the contract for the purpose of building a secretariat for the organization. As Alhaji Akingbola revealed, the secretariat had at the time of the interview cost the union seven million naira, and was located in Kelebe area of Osogbo. The secretariat represented, as the elderly man put it, the evidence of "the gain we realized from the contract given to us and is something that cannot be forgotten."

This writer paid a visit to the secretariat in Kelebe, Osogbo, on Saturday November 12, 2016. It was the day of the general meeting of the union and was thus able to interact with the members. They all spoke glowingly of the project, and the benefits they derived from it both individually and as an organization. A member of executive of the union gave information on how they got the project, the instructions they received at the start, how it was executed and the sense of gratitude they continued to nurse towards the administration:

> We were given the contract of designing OYES uniforms for both male and female; and were guided on how to go about it. We were given samples brought from Lagos. We were given some to show to our members: and they insisted that the job must be distributed among all members in Osun State without political or partisan considerations. They also wanted it to be spread to all Local Governments regardless of whether the tailors in any local government have remained

> active or not. We then realized that it was as beneficial for the association as it was for the members who had all the while become indifferent to the existence of the group. So, we ensured that the contract was extended to both members and non-members of the association in all Local Governments of the state. We monitored it closely. This influenced those who were not our members to take a decision to join us. This is the first out of many things for which we are very grateful to Ogbeni Aregbesola. He was completely non-sentimental about it. That really improved our collectivity. We were paid the right amount we charged for the work. We were not owed and we also did not disappoint them on the contract given us. One out of the many benefits that accrued to us from the project is the place where this meeting is holding.

Prince Akinloye, the current president of the union spoke on how the building of the hall was conceived and executed. According to him, the question of building a secretariat never occurred to them when they secured the first round of the contract. Rather, the money was simply paid to members who did the job as soon as it was received. When, however, the second batch arrived, it occurred to them all that it was necessary to do something that would serve as a permanent evidence of the important development. So, and to now quote the man, "we bought this piece of land, did the survey and commenced construction till it got to this stage."

III

A second group of tailors which got a share of the contract to design uniforms for OYES is the National Society of Professional Tailors (NSPT). The society is a breakaway faction from the Nigeria Union of Tailors. There are conflicting accounts as to how and why it broke away initially and this really is not of any real importance here. What is, lies in the fact of the association's involvement in the OYES project.

Prince Adewale Gay, who was president of the society between 2004 and 2012 admitted to this writer in an interview conducted with him in his shop in Osogbo on October 2, 2016 that, his own organization, compared to the Nigeria Union of Tailors, is a much smaller one, and that it had continued to have problem achieving recognition. In fact, as he further admitted, as at the time when the first batch of the contract was being given out, the government of the state of Osun was totally unaware of its existence and, this being so, did not make any provision for it when the contract was being awarded.

Adewale Gay said he swung into action as soon as he learned of the contract. He approached Alhaji Akingbola who, after consulting with other members of his own executive, simply offered to let go of a very tiny fraction of the contract. Adewale Gay returned to members of his own organization to inform them of what his efforts had yielded. They were all very angry with him, as he confessed, with many of them actually threatening to pull out of the society. They finally agreed to accept what had been offered, after all, and as the cliché goes, half a loaf is better than none. It is important to, at this point, listen to Adewale Gay's words directly. The man spoke to this writer in Yoruba but the English translation of what he said is presented immediately after the Yoruba original:

> Oun ti won fun wa ko ju one percent gbogbo ise ti won gba. Bo ya 1250 uniforms pere ni won fun wa. Kini yen de to bi almost forty-something thousand ni nkan ti won ko fun won. Because won fe ki omo kokan ni aso meji meji and they are working toward twenty thousand. Awon omo egbe ba mi ja. Egbe gan fe tu but Olohun ran mi lowo. Along the line, mo baa won kan s'oro. A gb'eyin lo s'alaye pe bo se ye ko ri niyi. Won wa ni lojo iwaju awon a mo nkan ti awon a se. Thanks to the people who are there now, people like Odulaja, that very young man…the Young…soldier kan wan'be…

ENGLISH TRANSLATION

> What they gave us was just about one percent of the job they got. They gave us, I think, 1250 uniforms to sew whereas the entire quantity was well over forty thousand. It was planned in such a way that each cadet member would have two uniforms each, and they had a plan to engage twenty thousand of them in the first batch. Our members were really angry with me; so much so that the association almost collapsed. But with the help of God, I was able to wade through the crisis. Along the line, I spoke with some individuals. We went behind to explain to the authorities that they had been misinformed. They promised that they would make amend in due course. Thanks to the people who are there now; people like Odulaja, the Young.. There was also one soldier among them…

The officers that Adewale Gay spoke with really kept their word. For, as he stated during the interview, the Nigeria Society of Professional Tailors was the first organization to be considered by the implementation committee when the second batch of the contract was being given out. This time around, they were given about five thousand uniforms to design. Members were happy and Adewale Gay himself regained respect as the leader of the society. The president spoke in very glowing terms about the gains made from the contract both at the personal and organizational levels. Again, he spoke in Yoruba but the English translation is provided immediately after the original:

> A dupe lowo Olohun. Majority awon omo egbe mi ni ipinle Osun ni won gba pe Olohun se iyanu fun won ni arin igba ti a ko aso yen de ti won ran because elomiin ti o ni ju machine eyo kan lo tele tele, won di oni machine meji. Elomiin mu tailoring material mo ise to n se. Lati ibi individually ni mo n so yen o. Leyin e, the society itself ri so many things nibe. Ekinni, ikan ni e si n wo ti won retain mi as president sibe yi: Cooperative. Nitori ni igba yen a da cooperative sile through achievement won. So, o le da owo si 'be, o si le gba owo ni 'be; kii owo yen ma baa tete tan ni owo awon omo to sise yen ni igba na.

TRANSLATION

> We thank God. Majority of our members in this state admitted that God performed wonders in their lives within the period when we were awarded the contract. Some who had only one sewing machine each were able to add a second one. Others decided to venture into sales of tailoring materials. All this was at the individual level. Because the society itself benefitted in many ways from the project. First, it was the project that made us to launch this cooperative society of which I am the president. We started it after having received our pay from the work we did. So, members could through it save money, or even obtain loans. With this, members won't just spend off any money they got.

IV

The third group of tailors who participated in the project of designing uniforms for OYES cadets is known as O'Tailors. Those comprising this group actually were people in whom the state had, one way or the other, invested by sponsoring them for short training in one vocation or the other. O'Tailor members were 112 in number and had participated in a three – month training programme in Sam and Sara, a fashion designing school located in Mowe, Ogun State. This was between December 2010 and February 2011 and at the expense of the government of the State of Osun.

Alhaja Mariam Olorunoje Rasheed who was the woman coordinator of the Osun participants on the training course gave detailed account of how they were selected for it during an interview I had with her in her Osogbo residence on October 22, 2016. According to her, the immediate reason which made the state government to take a decision to send them for the training was the introduction of the new uniforms in public schools in the state. It was considered important to have a competent pool of tailors who could simply be called upon to design the uniforms when eventually the decision was taken to introduce them. It was based on this consideration that they were invited to the State Secretariat, Abere and asked to present the certificates awarded them at the end of their initial training as tailors. Those who satisfied this condition were tested further by being asked to design sample uniforms and it was those who were considered to have passed this practical test that were then sent for further training at Sam and Sara, Mowe.

According to Alhaja Mariam Rasheed, the selection was based purely on merit, and not at all influenced by partisan considerations such as political party affiliation.

As indicated earlier, the cost of the training was borne by the state government. All participants on the course received full sponsorship, and this included course fees, accommodation costs and feeding allowances. As Alhaja Mariam Rasheed stated, Sam and Sara introduced them to state-of-the-art designing machines and they were also taught how to operate them. All those who underwent the course were issued certificates of participation at the end of the three – month training and they all returned to Osun with a new sense of confidence and pride. The OYES uniform designing project which they were invited to be part of a few months later served to put the training they received in Mowe to test.

Specifically on the OYES uniform designing contract, Alhaja Mariam Rasheed provided details of how she had received a call from Gbenga Odulaja, the man whom she said was in charge of the project, summoning her down to their operations office in Osogbo. She had invited three other members of the group to join her, and the four of them immediately drove down to the office. The implementation committee subjected them to a brief interview on their arrival at the OYES office. The officers were particularly concerned with whether they would be able to meet a deadline as short as three or four weeks if they were offered the job, a question to which they responded by saying yes. Two more visits after this and all paperwork had been completed. They went with a truck on the next visit to take delivery of fabrics for designing close to twenty (20) thousand uniforms. Alhaja Mariam gives extensive details of how they executed the contract in Yoruba but the English translation is provided immediately after the original:

> Nigba ti a koko pe ara wa pe won ma ni ka lo mu moto wa, awon kan ni nkan elo ni won fe fun wa ti won ni ki a lo wa moto. La ba gbe moto nla de. Akoko won load ise, eekeji a ba ri ibi ja ise si mo, a ba ja si ile mi nibi. A a le ja si shop ki won ma lo ko aso alaso lo. Mo ja sibi, mo ja si shop co-ordinator, a ba pe gbogbo wa jo. Gbogbo omo egbe pata pata. Tori gbogbo each local government lo wa laarin wa. Awon to wa lati Ila, Ijebu-Jesha. A sha pe everybody, oju gbogbo wa pe. A wa wo pe bawo la se fe se. Won de ti fun wa lojo. A wa lo si shop man kan, Shop meji lohun gba, shop tie tobi. Awon ti a mo pe won je oga ise, ti won danto, a ko ti won fun won,

> won ko lo si shop pelu sample. Awa yoku, a sa ara wa jo, a wa submit machine. A ko machine jo bayi, eni to ni weaving machine, bi a se de, eni to ti ra machine eyokan, machine ti a ri nigba ti a lo sise yen, onina ni. Eniti o ra, a ko jo, awa kan wa nge aso, o di rinran. So time ti won de fun wa, inu mi dun pe a o fail, ti a fi lo submit ise yen, inu won dun gan.
>
> ENGLISH TRANSLATION
>
> When we informed our members that we have been told to go and hire a lorry to move the materials for the project being awarded us, most of us thought it was mere exaggeration. When we eventually managed to collect the materials, we were confronted with the challenge of where to store them. It was then agreed that the consignment be brought to my house here. We could not afford to take it to the shop for fear of theft. We brought some of the consignments here and took others to the coordinator's shop. Then we called our members from all the Local Governments to deliberate on how to complete the job on schedule; because we were given a deadline. We decided to do the job in one of our member's shop. He has an adjoining shop that makes his place spacious enough for our use. The most senior members took their shares first which they took to their shops along with samples. For the rest of us, we collected machines from all our members. Everyone was encouraged to bring along whatever machines they had. So, as some of us cut the fabrics into pieces, others were busy sewing them. I am so pleased that we turned in the work before the stipulated deadline expired.

As Alhaja Mariam Olorunoje Rasheed says, O'Tailor members prized highly the training course they underwent in Mowe and the certificates they were issued with following the completion of the training. The school, she argued, was well known all over the world and what this means was that they could secure job wherever they went with the certificates they now held. With regards to the OYES contract, she spoke glowingly of the benefits that her members derived from it. Some she said bought small parcels of land from what they were able to make from it and started working on it immediately while others who had abandoned building projects were able to resume work on them and complete them. Many members spent part of the proceeds to get new equipment for their shops and their trades, as she said, had since then continued to boom. Finally, as she submitted, OYES project provided them with the opportunity to put the training they had received into practice. With it, they were thus able to develop great confidence in themselves. This, she said, was what all members appreciated most of all the other benefits they derived from the contract.

V

It is time to move on to a second category of artisans who benefitted from OYES programme. These are the shoe makers or shoe manufacturers, depending on the term preferred. It was this class of professionals who made the boots which OYES volunteers wore to complement the uniforms.

This writer spoke with Alhaji Ganiyu Adekunle, president of the Osun Shoemakers Association in his workshop in Osogbo. According to him, his association did not know anything about the boots given to the first batch of OYES volunteers and that they saw the shoes for the first time when the cadets moved on to the streets at the end of the three-week training course. They felt flabbergasted when, on enquiry, they were told that the shoes were brought in from Aba. They decided to make immediate representations to the implementation committee of the programme letting them know that they were fully competent to make such shoes. They were asked to supply samples and they did. They were then asked to make another twelve (12) pairs which again they did. The implementation committee was really impressed by what it saw and thus asked the shoemakers to produce another 200 pairs. Again, the numbers were turned in, in no time. By this time, the committee had been won over completely. It took a decision to award the shoemakers a contract to manufacture 7000 pairs of shoes.

It was the biggest contract the association had ever won in the history of its existence, according to Alhaji Adekunle. And what he did immediately after securing it was to contact all branch coordinators in all the local governments within the state. As soon as they had assembled, the project was presented to them and a decision was taken on how to share them out. The seven thousand pairs of shoes were ready in no time, and a second contract was awarded them as soon as the first one was delivered. This time, they were asked to make six thousand pairs. After this, a third one came and it was for another seven thousand pairs. This meant that altogether, the association made twenty thousand (20,000) pairs of shoes for OYES.

As Alhaji Adekunle stated during the interview, what impressed his members most about the job was the prompt payment of the money involved. As he put it, his association never experienced any delay before receiving payment for the job done. Seventy percent of whatever amount was agreed upon was always paid as soon as a contract had been awarded while the remaining thirty percent got paid once the work had been completed. What is more: they were paid all the time in cash, and never by cheque! Alhaji Adekunle was modest when it came to speaking about the gains made by his members from the project. He expressed himself in Yoruba but an English translation of his statement is provided immediately after the Yoruba original.

> A dupe lowo Olorun. Toro kobo ti kaluku wa ri gege bi anfani, ko si eni ti ko ri ope du. Olorun ma je ki a dupe ibanuje. Gbogbo wa ti a se ise yi,bi o ti je ise opo, la ri wipe awa tiwantiwa, tori to ba je wipe egbe wa, a mo iye ti a le gba pair kookan. Sugbon nigbati o ti je wipe awon omo wa naa ni won fi gba sise, won o ma rindin kaakiri mo, awa naa ba won fi owo so owo po, a o woju mo wipe dandan a gbodo gba iye bayi. A gba less, o si pe wa nitori pe ise pe meta: ki eeyan gba ise ki o sooti, eni niyen, ki o gba ise ki o bo si oju deede, eji niyen, ki o gba ise, ki o ri iwonba tie, Olorun je ki a ri iwonba tiwa.

ENGLISH TRANSLATION

> We thank God. Every member who participated in the job was able to make something small out of it and we were all happy about it. May we always have good things to thank God for. We deliberately drew back from charging exorbitantly for the project. This is simply because of our belief that it was our own job. We know government was trying to assist us by creating employment for our children such that they would stop roaming the streets, and it was because of this that we made it cheap for OYES. But we were still able to make a modest profit at the end of the day. You know there are three kinds of jobs: some are done at a loss, others you just manage to break even but there are others where you just make a little profit. We thank God that we were able to make small profits out of this particular job.

But while Alhaji Ganiyu Adekunle might have been somewhat restrained in giving expression to the kind of benefits he and his members derived from the contracts awarded his association, he nonetheless demonstrated a sense of understanding of the greater goal of the Osun Youth Empowerment Scheme. As evident from his response quoted above, Alhaji Adekunle believes that OYES is meant to provide employment for young men and women of Osun State – indeed their own children. Later on in the course of the interview, he expressed deep appreciation for the decision to introduce such a scheme.

VI

Alhaji Musibau Isola is the chairman of BRIMAC Industries, a shoe manufacturing company which otherwise is known as MUSI Shoes. The company which was located in Iwo was first opened for business in 1989. Prior to setting it up, Alhaji Isola had for long been involved in foot wear business, travelling to Italy and other European countries from where he imported shoes. BRIMAC was a very modern establishment and a relatively large company. At the time when it was operating at full capacity, it used to produce about 3000 shoes per day.

Business started going down for BRIMAC at the point when the Federal Government took a decision to allow Chinese companies import shoes into the country. At first, the level of importation was only a little more than a trickle but this increased progressively until it reached a point when it could now be described as an invasion. By 2007, things had become so bad for BRIMAC and this was to the extent that it now had to lay off most of its workers. With time, even those who were allowed to stay back also had to be placed on contract employment, the implication being that they would be invited back only when the company succeeded in its struggles to win contracts.

This writer interviewed Alhaji Musibau Isola, the chairman of the company on February 1, 2017 in the workshop at Iwo. Alhaji Isola told him that it was in the course of running around, exploring ways of keeping the company afloat that he stumbled on the information concerning OYES shoe-making contract. He said he quickly moved to contact key members of the implementation committee who, by way of initial reaction, asked him to present the certificate of his company's incorporation. This was absolutely no problem. Next he was asked to bring samples, This again he did. Finally, a representation of the implementation committee comprising the commandante, Gbenga Odulaja and Kola Omotunde-Young travelled down to Iwo to inspect the factory. Impressed by what they saw, they agreed to award him the contract but only if he could present a bank guarantee. Again, he had no problem doing this. About three months later, he received advance payment for the supply of five thousand (5000) pairs of shoes. Alhaji Isola quickly summoned his men and work commenced. The interview I had with him is in Yoruba but the English translation of the excerpt below is provided immediately after the Yoruba original:

> Nigba ti a nise gan an ni a to won awon osise pada. A ni permanent staff; koda a ni quarters fun won. Ise n lo deede

> nigba yen. Sugbon nigba to ya ti Chinese bere si ni ko bata wo'le lo di boo lo o ya fun mi. Ni gbogbo e wa daru. Emi ni Bata, won o rise se mo. Gbogbo shoe industry; a mo'ra wa. A de so fun awon oga OYES pe ise ti e fe gbe sita yi a le se gbogbo e ti won ba le fun wa. Won de so pe awon maa pin fun gbogbo awon ti won n se bata inu ile alafowose se.
>
> ENGLISH TRANSLATION
>
> It was after we got the job that we recalled the staff. We used to have permanent staff and even staff quarters. At that time, there was work to do. Things became bad when the Chinese began to import foot wears into the country. All the shoe manufacturers went out of business. We know each other very well – I mean all of us in shoe manufacturing business. We actually told the implementation committee that our company has the capacity to handle the entire project but they insisted on sharing it in such a way as to accommodate all those who bided for it.

The first five thousand pairs were delivered within three weeks, following which they were awarded a second contract. This time, it was for seven thousand (7000) pairs. This too was delivered within deadline. Alhaji Isola was quick to add that on its side too, the implementation committee never broke its promise to settle the balances once the shoes had been delivered. He expressed deep satisfaction with what his company was able to make from the contract. Beyond this, the benefits, he said, was enjoyed also by his workers and, as well, the people of Iwo. It is important to listen to him directly as he spoke in Yoruba. As usual, an English translation will be provided immediately after the Yoruba original:

> Ise ti won fun wa, ere ti a ri nbe ki Olorun fi alubarika si. But to ba se pe a fe gba lodo won ka se dada…o keep ile ise wa busy nigba yen na. Awon kan de tun sise n be to se pe awon ri tiwon naa nbe. Tori eni ti e pe ko wa sise, to gba owo e lasiko, yi o maa s'adua fun yin ni. So, nigba yen, awon omo Iwo - ilu wa - awon na jere oselu
>
> ENGLISH TRANSLATION
>
> We are truly satisfied with the gains we made from the job that was given to us. But if we had been allowed to make

> the shoes according to our own standard… meanwhile, the contract kept our company engaged at the time, and those who worked with us made something from it too. Of course, anyone who is invited to work and is paid on time will be grateful for such an opportunity. Even the people of Iwo, our town, also indirectly, enjoyed the dividend of democracy.

Just like Alhaji Adekunle, Alhaji Musibau Isola praised the state government for the decision to launch OYES. Employment creation, as he said, is a primary responsibility of any government, and at any level. Seeing young people who were hitherto unemployed doing one thing or the other on a daily basis made him feel really happy. This way, they would at least be able to take something home at the end of each month. This, as he says, is by far better than giving people handouts of two or three thousand naira, and engaging them as thugs and/or bodyguards.

VII

The artisans that have been fore grounded as secondary beneficiaries of OYES in this chapter are only representative. They do not exhaust the list of such workers which executed one contract or the other for the scheme between 2011 and 2013. There were, for example, artists and sign writers who designed logos for the scheme and prepared badges for the uniforms. There also were small scale traders from whom working tools like cutlasses, rakes, hoes, brooms, packers and so on were procured. Even for tailors, there was at least one other association which also benefitted from the uniform designing contracts but which has not been cited here. It was known as Nigeria Federation of Tailors.

In short, the point being made here is that the ones who have come up for discussion in the foregoing pages are simply examples, and that their experiences were replicated in several other instances. It is also that the concept of empowerment which is central to OYES has, at a secondary level, been extended to these common run of workers some of whom do not even have basic education. Take the case of the Nigeria Union of Tailors. I have pointed out that, and as Alhaji Akingbola stated during my interview with him, prior to the OYES job, members were already losing interest in the umbrella body. As soon as the union won the contract however, their faith in it became automatically renewed. Now, they even had a secretariat which all of them feel proud to identify with. This is empowerment at the organizational level. And even though the Nigeria Society of Professional Tailors was not able to complete work on its own secretariat, it was at least able to launch a cooperative society. Through it, members could begin to make savings. They could also obtain loans from it. This is another instance of empowerment at the organizational level.

The benefits individual artisans derived from the contracts is also quite substantial. In the interview I had with her, Alhaja Mariam Olorunoje Rasheed pointed out how several members of her organization used part of what they were able to make from the job to procure parcels of land which they started developing immediately, or how some who had earlier abandoned their building projects returned to them as soon as they got paid for the job they did. Some were also said to have purchased additional equipment. Adewale Gay, on his own, cited examples of such things which his members achieved at the individual levels after having executed the job given to them, how some procured additional sewing machines while others ventured into selling accessories. Alhaji Musibau Isola says that nothing made him as happy these days as seeing the machines at BRIMAC Industries roaring to life. OYES project achieved that for him in 2013. Since then, he had won contracts from the Nigeria Police Force and the Prisons Service. As it happened though, the machines had after completing the jobs, had to go silent again.

The temptation to go on is strong but the point to make is that the hope which OYES offered was not just to the youths of the state which represented its primary target. Rather, it was extended as well to several other classes of people – ordinary people. For these people, a situation where a state government would offer contracts relating directly to their areas of professional competence had no historical precedent. Virtually everybody I interviewed in this regard made this clear. Although the state was not able to sustain it, the beneficiaries remained ever grateful, nonetheless.

CHAPTER SIX

CONCLUSION: OYES FOR THE FUTURE

OYES started off on an ambitious note – and this is meant in the sense of the number of volunteers it engaged when it first took off. Osun State civil service had only 18000 staff as at January 2011. Yet, when the same state launched the youth empowerment programme, it did so with 20,000 volunteers. This is a remarkable feat, especially when the fact is considered that the state in question is severely limited in resources. Indeed, of all the thirty-six states that constitute the Nigerian federation, Osun receives the third littlest amount from the monthly federal allocation.

Even when placed on a global comparative index, employing 20,000 people at one go would still be considered as a great feat. Actually, most countries who had attempted such programmes usually commenced enlistments with far more modest figures – say, five or six thousand. Guardedly then, it can be argued that the figure 20,000 remains almost totally unprecedented in the history of youth engagement anywhere in the world. This is all the more so when it is considered that OYES as a programme was introduced by just one out of the thirty-six units that constitute the Nigerian federation.

Not long after OYES took off, several other states in the federation started to express curiosity in the programme. They started putting voice to their intention to introduce similar youth engagement schemes in their different domains. The commandante, in the interview I had with him, put the number of the states who expressed such interests at eighteen. These, according to him, included Cross Rivers, Rivers, Borno, Kano, Kaduna, Niger, Ekiti, and Ondo. As he further stated in the interview, not many were able to carry through with the plans while even those who did could not sustain it. What was lacking as he saw it, were the important factors of discipline, dedication and commitment.

Femi Ifaturoti actually provided some details on the efforts made by Ekiti and Oyo states to introduce youth employment schemes in their respective states, following the example set by OYES.

In the case of Oyo State, the deputy governor of the state had invited OYES officials down to Ibadan. Four people, including Ifaturoti himself, Kola Omotunde-Young and the commandante went on the trip. They held a meeting with the deputy governor of the state together with the Chief of Staff and the state Commissioner for Youths, Sports and Development. Following the visit, the state commenced the process of introducing a scheme tagged YESO (Youth Employment Scheme of Oyo State). In doing so, they followed closely the advice which the OYES team provided them with. The scheme eventually took off with 10,000 cadets. When the economic downturn set in, they reduced the number of the cadets to 5000. Oyo State continued to run the employment scheme for upward of five years. The only thing is that it never came near the scale of that of OYES.

As things stand at the present moment, Oyo state seemed to be the only other state that was able to launch and sustain an employment programme out of the other thirty-five states of the federation.

A second state would probably have been Ekiti. Unfortunately, however, the programme could not take off because of the unexpected change in government. As could be inferred from the discussion I had with Femi Ifaturoti, Kayode Fayemi, the immediate past governor of the state who subsequently became the Minister for Solid Minerals appeared to be serious about going into the programme. His failure to secure a second term in the gubernatorial election of April 2014 seemed to be the factor that put paid to the plan.

With regards however to the rest of the states that expressed interests in launching such a scheme, it appeared that the reason why the efforts failed to yield fruits lies in the fact of the inability of those charged with implementing it to follow with diligence, the advice made available to them by those in charge of implementing the Osun model. This much can be inferred from both the submissions of Femi Ifaturoti and Col. Eniibukun Oyewole (rtd) in this regard.

But the World Bank also came calling. Well, right from the onset, and as it had earlier been stated, the Bretton Wood institution demonstrated an attitude of goodwill toward OYES. Its initial response when the programme just took off was to delegate some of its officers to closely observe it and monitor its progress. As time went on, its officials began to get fascinated by the way it was being implemented. Two things impressed the country head most in the way the programme was being run. First was the energy and honesty of purpose of members of the implementation committee and second, the complete transparency in the method of payment of stipends to beneficiaries. The institution continued to note down its observations as the programme continued to make progress, even as it compared it to other empowerment programmes in other developing countries, including Pakistan, Rwanda, Tanzania and Brazil. It also decided to make these observations available to members of the implementation committee. Soon it would start sending some of these officers on tour of these other countries. In July 2012 for example, World Bank sponsored the trio of commandante, Col. Oyewole (rtd), Gbenga Odulaja and Diran Fashesin on a one-week trip to Rwanda to observe that country's own programme of youth empowerment. Not long after, and based on the copious notes it had taken while observing the implementation of OYES, the World Bank began to think of launching its own youth empowerment programme for the entire Nigerian federation. It was to go by the name Youth Empowerment and Social Support Operations (YESSO).

YESSO was yet to take off as at the moment of sending this book to press but the plans, as I gathered, were now in the final stages. While it is important not to confuse it with the Osun Youth Empowerment Scheme which represents the subject of this book, it is still important to highlight some of its point of departures.

Like the model which inspired it, YESSO is designed to have a two-part programme for its beneficiaries: the first, which will be primary, will be in form of community service; and the second, vocational training, will be secondary. However, unlike OYES which sets the minimum educational qualification at

WASCE, YESSO aims to have as its target those who, in the economic sense, can be guardedly described as extremely poor and vulnerable. Drawing from the pool of knowledge it has gathered in the course of monitoring such programmes in different countries, World Bank came to the conclusion that the educational attainment of the poorest of the poor never went beyond a maximum of nine years of schooling. Most often, as the institution further contended, they are complete illiterates. It was based on this therefore that it set the highest educational qualifications of would-be beneficiaries of its own programme at JSS 3. Thirdly, and perhaps surprisingly, World Bank is of the view that the amount paid to individual volunteers by OYES is relatively on the high side. For YESSO beneficiaries, the monthly stipend would likely be between five and seven thousand naira only.

As it would seem, it is the issues which World Bank took with the manner of implementation of OYES that now came to constitute the core difference between the initiative of the state of Osun known as Osun Youth Empowerment Programme and the one it is now trying to introduce and which is named Youth Empowerment and Social Support Operations.

But perhaps, the greatest point of departure of YESSO lies in the decision by the World Bank to introduce what has been described as Community Based Targeting (CBT). Directly, Community Based Targeting aims to prepare a comprehensive social register of the poor in a given state or, to put it technically, design a poverty map of the state's population.

Once a good poverty map has been created, the next step in YESSO will be to identify the six poorest local government areas in the state, two from each of the three senatorial districts. Following this, the officers in charge of the operations will now have to step down, practically, and relocate to the identified communities. Their mission would be to identify households that are considered ultra-poor, using local criteria. Gbenga Odulaja, head of the implementation unit of YESSO in the state of Osun explains the process of recruitment of beneficiaries for YESSO in an interview with this writer:

> And when you get to those communities you gather the youths separately, you gather the women separately, you gather the elders separately and you ask them, what do you think poverty is all about? How would they identify a poor person in their community? The indices may be different from community to community. For instance, if you are from the north, if your father does not have two or three

> goats, or he does not have a specified number of cows, he is likely to be categorized among the extremely poor and vulnerable. Poverty has to be measured in accordance with local people's own criteria. At the end of the day, the youths will bring their own list, the women will bring their own list and the elders will bring their own. You now look at all the lists together. You will see some names that cut across, names that are recurring; you now agree that these ones have been agreed upon by everybody as poor households. It is those poor households that you go to. You take the data of every one in there: their age, their profession and everything. They don't know what you want to do with it. You put it in your computer. The process of creating a data base has begun.

As Odulaja further explained, it is from the data base thus created that the list of beneficiaries would be drawn. He provided details of the challenges they found themselves confronted with while compiling the list of participants, stating that when they applied the criteria set by World Bank to the first six local governments, the result they got was a list of less than 600 people. This being the case, World Bank allowed them to add the next six local governments, making twelve – four from each senatorial district. It was by virtue of this grace that they were now able to get enough number of people on their list, enough for them to take off.

It is important to add that Community Based Targeting does not end with collecting data from communities and identifying extremely poor households among them. Part of its dimension includes the fact that it is the local people themselves who would suggest the kind of service they would need from the youths that are to be engaged: the local people are the ones to tell YESSO managers what their urgent needs are - be it access roads, toilets, wells, storage facilities for their harvests, etc, etc. Beneficiaries are expected to work on putting in place the infrastructural facilities that have been demanded by the communities. They are expected to do this four times a week, working for four hours a day. The rest of the time is to be spent with the youths learning a skill or vocation. The trade could be one that a beneficiary has started training in before but which he/she has had to abandon due to lack of finances, or one that he/she has always been interested in but has never really been able to devote time to. On graduation, a beneficiary is supposed to procure the equipment needed to practise the trade and become self-employed. The inspiration provided by OYES in this regard is clear but there is no harm in re-stating it.

When the World Bank first made known its plan to introduce a youth engagement programme in Nigeria, at least eighteen states of the federation immediately announced their intention to be part of it. But then, the institution made known its eligibility criteria, the most primary of them being that any state that wanted to participate ought to have a social support programme that it has been running. Such programme, as the eligibility criterion further makes clear, must have been on ground for nothing less than two years, and must have a budget line and a process that ensures due diligence. The World Bank insisted on verifying the claims made by each of the states in this regard and, in the process, a number of the states were eliminated.

Secondly, World Bank also insisted that the participating states must take responsibility for a percentage of the allowances to be paid to the beneficiaries. Initially, and as Gbenga Odulaja stated, this support was fixed at fifty percent. Later, having been made aware of the economic difficulties confronting many of the states, the World Bank reviewed the percentage downward, reducing it to thirty. It however insisted that each intending state must be ready to deposit the twelve-month equivalent of this thirty percent in a designated account even before the programme takes off. Again, many states could not meet this condition. Thus, it has happened that YESSO will be taking off with eight states in the first instance. In addition to Osun, the other states are Cross River, Ekiti, Oyo, Kwara, Bauchi, Niger, Kogi. Again, for the state of Osun, Femi Ifaturoti was appointed the coordinator of State Operation Coordinating Unit (SOCU) while Gbenga Odulaja, as stated before, was to serve as the head of the implementation unit. Other officers on the programme are Femi Oyedele, Project Officer, Training, Ibrahim Kamoru, Monitoring and Evaluation Officer, and Tayo Odugbile, Head of Administration. Again, as it ought to be made clear, the World Bank employment project, at least as far as it concerns the State of Osun, remains dependent on the structures already established by OYES.

II

I opened this book by providing background information on the vision that propelled the introduction of OYES. I wrote of a number of groups of idealists whose membership overlapped with each other. Finally, I settled on PFG which simply was a group of five people of which Rauf Aregbesola was a member. It was this group of five which wrote a small green book titled "My Pact with the People of Osun State". The Yoruba version of the book was published back to back with the English version and is titled "Majemu mi Pelu awon Eniyan mi ni Ipinle Osun". The book contains "six integral action plans" that the group sought to implement in the State of Osun should it win the

2007 governorship election in the state through Rauf Aregbesola. The third of these action plans is a pledge to create 20,000 jobs for the youths of the state within the first one hundred days in office. Osun Youth Empowerment Scheme (OYES) served as the transformation of that plan into action.

In addition to tackling unemployment problem in the state, it was the intention of PFG members to, through the programme, establish a model of youth employment that could be emulated both nationally and globally. OYES provided that example to a considerable extent, and it is in an attempt to prove this that I have earlier on in this chapter sought to give details of the efforts made by a number of other states of the federation to establish their own versions of the employment scheme. It is also the reason why I have presented some details of the outline of YESSO, the version which the World Bank is now trying to introduce.

I stated in chapter two that only about ten percent or less of those who applied for placement were offered employment in the first batch. At the same time, I also stated in the same chapter that OYES reduced the rate of employment in the State of Osun to less than three percent. There is a contradiction somewhere, isn't it? This precisely is the reason why I promised to return to the issue in this concluding chapter.

So how did ten percent of a total number of applicants achieve so much difference as to cut the rate of unemployment in the state sharply to a mere three percent? Well, the answer will be clear if we consider the following. One, all candidates who had a first degree or even higher qualifications were positively considered for employment. Two, all candidates with HND in 27 out of the 30 local government areas in the state were also offered employment. Finally, at least 80% of all candidates with NCE also had their applications positively considered. What this means, in other words, is that most of the candidates who had qualifications that made them employable were engaged by OYES. A second reason that contributed to the fact of the sharp decline in the rate of unemployment in the state is the policy that deliberately ensured that money earned by OYES cadets was also spent or invested in the state. In other words, those who secured employment under OYES and started small scale businesses with their savings also automatically became employers, so to say. Finally, and this is related to the second point above, there is the ramification of opportunities offered by information technology in the process of OYES recruitment. I stated in chapter two that when it was discovered that application forms were being hoarded by some civil servants in the state, the implementation committee decided to create a website (www.oyes.org.ng) from where applicants could download the forms directly. This immediately removed the artificial scarcity but perhaps more importantly, also increased the level of awareness of the potentials of the internet in the state. What this means is that cyber cafes started springing up everywhere as applicants struggled to download the forms. Also, those among them – and the number was large - who hitherto never had email addresses immediately opened accounts for themselves and started running them. This was to the extent that by the time the process of recruitment for the second batch in 2013 commenced, the implementation committee had acquired sufficient confidence as to make it decide to make internet the only source of access to anything that has to do with OYES. All applications were filed through the internet. Photographs and other important data were uploaded through the internet. Biometric verifications were carried out using digital technology. Certificates were verified using the same technology. Since patronage was now very high, more and more cyber cafes kept on being established. Several young men and women of the state also secured employment in these cafes.

The development was of course consistent with the ultimate aim of OYES, which was to inculcate in the beneficiaries the virtues of self reliance and make them believe in the real meaning of the word "apalara" - the main title of this book – which, simply translated, means that real salvation lies in the strength of an individual's arms. In other words, OYES sought to make the youth of Osun understand the importance of self belief and self dependence. During the three – week training programme which preceded deployment, and as explained in chapter three, efforts were made to prepare the cadets psychologically and mentally for this reality through the lessons; and physically through the drills and exercises. The rudimentary lessons in history were meant to make the volunteers understand themselves and their different societies, while the topics in economics and politics were designed to give them a grasp of power and economic relations in the world.

The focus of chapter four is on deployment and exit programmes. Seven areas of deployment are identified and discussed, and it is pointed out how OYES worked in cooperation with different arms and agencies of government in the state. One point that needs to be stressed again is this: OYES offered the youths of the state hopes afresh. It provided them a means of sustenance for two years and, at the end, made them learn one form of trade or the other, and through which they could individually continue to sustain themselves. But it was also the case that while the programme lasted, these youths also rendered invaluable services to the state. They kept the streets clean, cleared wastes, assisted in road rehabilitation, helped in controlling traffic, and served as auxiliary teachers in schools. The point being made here is that the two broad parties involved in the scheme derive mutual benefits from it. And saying this should not be interpreted as an attempt to take anything away from the achievement of OYES. On the contrary, the point actually helped to further underline the depth of thoughts that went into the process of the scheme's conception.

In focusing on the artisans who were brought in to render different kinds of services to the scheme in chapter five, efforts were made to highlight the benefits derived by these low - income earning workers at the individual as well as the organizational levels. But perhaps the most remarkable thing about the involvement of this category of professionals lies precisely in the fact that it was the first time ever that they would be having an opportunity to participate in a project with the government of the state. It was a good development in one sense. But it is also sad that up till that point, it never occurred to any of the earlier administrations to enter into any kind of productive engagement with the mass of artisans in the state.

II

OYES was able to inaugurate only two batches of 20,000 cadets each before the economic crisis set in. These were those of 2011-2013 and 2013 -2015.

Following the crisis, the implementation committee decided to go into what the commandante would describe as the "ad hoc mode". Simply, what is meant here is that the scheme had to cut down on some of its normal protocols, including processes of recruitment, training and inauguration. The total number of cadets taken on at any point also had to be reduced to just 6000, and the duration of service to six months. The implementation committee first went into this mode in 2015, and as at the time of winding up on this book, the scheme had turned out a total of six batches. A good percentage of those who benefited from this ad hoc alternative had also earlier participated as volunteers in the first two full batches. This means that, for long after the first two batches, not many fresh young men and women of the state were admitted into the scheme. Fortunately, and as was reliably gathered, a plan was being hatched to commence the process of recruitment of a new batch of volunteers. If this could be realised it clearly, would be a good development.

When I put it to Ambassador Otunla during an interview I had with him in his residence in Ikeja, Lagos, that it seemed the economic crisis was threatening the continuity of the OYES scheme, he responded by saying that it had never been easy anywhere "managing scarcity." As he contended, what happened, was that the big uncle who was giving out "free money has gone broke." Ambassador Otunla considered it really important to introduce fiscal federalism in the country, to "restructure the country, giving control to each state over its resources." Right then, as he thought, the crisis that occurred in Osun, and which was affecting not just OYES but rather all projects, was inevitable: "If your uncle is sending you to school, if your uncle gets bankrupt, you may have to stop going to school."

Ambassador Otunla lamented even more the fact that Subsistence Agriculture, the twin project to OYES as conceptualized by PFG, did not take off. He described the programme with a Yoruba word "S'agbedoba". As conceived then, and going by the implication of the Yoruba term, the programme was intended to turn ordinary farmers into kings.

Osun is a poor state, said Ambassador Otunla. This being the case, and as he further stated, it has nothing: "it is a peasant state like Arkansas in the United States, poor, dirty and poor. And one of the plans of PFG was to create wealth out of subsistence agriculture and we have not done that." In summary, the original plan, concerning subsistence agriculture, is to encourage peasant farmers to concentrate on planting food crops like vegetables, bananas, plantains, cassava, yams, maize, etc in large quantities; and to have licensing agents "who government will support by buying these things from them every morning so that they can go home with 2000 naira a day." It would have been such a great development, according to Ambassador Otunla, if the state had been able to pump some money into the project, encouraging small time farmers "to bring products from the farm, helping them to market such things in Lagos, enriching them by creating wealth at the bottom of the pyramid..."

I believe Ambassador Otunla had a good point. And for those who might wish to dismiss him as just another idealist or dreamer, my advice is that we return to what OYES was able to achieve in such a short period of time. In chapters three and four, I included testimonies from some of the people whose hopes OYES helped to re-kindle, whose lives the programme transformed. They included those who, through the scheme, succeeded in acquiring free training in different vocations; those who, like Toyin Adeleke, Iskilu Bolarinwa and the over 5000 qualified teachers working with SUBEB, who secured permanent appointment with the state; and those like Jamiu Ibrahim who were able to further their education through what they managed to save while serving as OYES cadets.

Simbiat Ilyasu, as she told this writer in an interview was abandoned by her husband simply because all the three children she had for him were females. But her continued ability to cater for herself and the three children, including taking care of their school fees was as a consequence of the allowance she earned as an OYES volunteer. Some like Sheriffdeen Sulaiman invested their savings in commercial motor cycles. Others preferred the transport mini buses popularly known in Osogbo and its environs as "korope". Twenty-nine or so of the beneficiaries even managed to build themselves each a bungalow in which they lived. Jamiu Ibrahim was one of such. And, as has been stated earlier, the way in which different categories of artisans in the state were brought into the scheme has no precedence in the history of the state.

In short, the point I am making is that the programme on Subsistence Agriculture which Ambassador Otunla felt passionate about may really be quite feasible. Since farming, as the man stressed, represents the occupation of majority of the people in the state, the main challenge that the government might have been confronted with would have been that of how to get the products directly from those who produced them in the villages and transporting them to large markets in places like Lagos and Abuja. This would have been similar to what the Commodity Board did with cocoa in the period immediately following independence. But it may probably be unfair to declaim with authority on the state's policy on Subsistence Agriculture in a book on OYES. This, not least because one may not have the full picture.

In moving on from this point therefore, all I want to add is that the way the programme on Subsistence Agriculture was conceived makes it appear like a fantastic complement to OYES. Combined together, and had adequate resources been available, the two could have gone a long way in the process of reducing alienation between government and citizens.

For the future, I want to even go so far as to recommend that government tries the idea of encouraging different classes of people and professionals in the state to constitute themselves into different forms of cooperatives. The cooperatives can then work with, and for each other, as well as with, and for, the state. For example, those in building and construction cooperatives, including bricklayers, block makers, plumbers, carpenters, etc can execute jobs for the state and/or its agencies, and I mean at a mass level as was the case with the artisans who were drafted to participate in the OYES projects. For the things they require for such a job, the traders' cooperatives will be ready to supply them. From whatever profits that may accrue from any such project executed by any of the cooperatives, a fraction will go to the state, another to the cooperative involved, while the rest will be shared among individual members. What this means is that for every single project a cooperative society wins, its members would simultaneously be working for themselves, their organization and the government of the state. With time, each cooperative would have saved enough that it could use to execute any project that it accepts to go into.

For those who may consider such a situation unrealisable, let me make it clear that I am not saying anything new. Iskilu Bolarinwa, one of those who were sent to Cuba on the sponsorship of OYES reported on what he observed of the agricultural system in the small island country. In an interview with Adetokunbo Shittu, Bolarinwa spoke glowingly of the strong spirit of self dependence which obtains among the people, the culture of maintenance and, with specific reference to the position that I am currently canvassing, the sharing formula. At this point, I would like to quote Iskilu Bolarinwa directly. He spoke in Yoruba but an English translation of what he said is provided immediately after the Yoruba original.

> a tun se research debi wipe the union leaders, bi won se je union yen won tun ni farm land: hectares of farm lands ni each province ti won de gba workers sibe. At the end of the day ti won ba harvest ti won ba ta ni international market gain ti won ba ri nibe, won a divide e into three: won de ma ko percentage kan fun government, awon na ma share percentage kan and the other third one won ma share fun awon workers.
>
> ENGLISH TRANSLATION
>
> ... we also discovered that the Union leaders practice agriculture regardless of their being unionists. They have

> farm lands: hectares of farm lands in each province, worked on by paid employees. At the end of each harvest, the produce is sold at the international market and the proceed is shared into three with a percentage going to the government, another to the coffers of the union leaders to be shared as appropriate and the third going to the payment of the worker's.

I have gone into all this in order to underline my position on the workability of my suggestion on how to sustain a laudable programme involving relatively large sections of the populace like OYES. It seems to me that in introducing the scheme, the brains behind it never envisaged the possibility of an economic crisis, and therefore never thought of finding an independent source of funding for it. In a dependent capitalist economic system that Nigeria operates, the kind of crisis that we have witnessed, and which has now almost completely scuffled OYES, and which prevented the take off of the sister project in subsistence farming, is in my view inevitable. The inability to take this reality on board and thus plan for the long term, may yet represent the major flaw in the conception and execution of most laudable projects in Nigeria. To resuscitate OYES, and keep it going for a long time, and indeed for the successful inauguration of other projects that might entail the involvement of a section of the masses of the citizens of the state, it will be necessary to consider ab initio a method that will, at the very least, make the participants in the project at least part owners of it. Saying this however does not represent an attempt to take anything away from what the Aregbesola government was able to achieve through the Osun Youth Empowerment Scheme.

APPENDIX I

IROGBO DECLARATION

THE PHILOSOPHY & PRINCIPLES OF PEOPLE FRIENDLY GOVERNANCE

BY ENGR. RAUF ADESOJI (ORANMIYAN ATUNLUSE)

World time can be configured in four stages, the pre-historic, the ancient, the modern and post modern. In all these stages, human societies have organized governance (order & progress) along two broad lines. The one on class interest the other protecting the general interest. In this post modern era, democracy aptly defined by President Abraham Lincoln as government of the people, by the people, for the people, has become the widely accepted & stoutly defended mark of civilization and good governance.

Democracy unfortunately has become a mechanistic numbers' game as power moves and is held on the basis of organized partisanship, electoral scheming & system which have enthroned first past the post victories instead of the general interest of the governed.

After close to thirty years of military intervention in Governance, Nigeria returned to democracy in 1999 but remains in the grip of serious challenges to the general interest.

President Olusegun Obasanjo has become historically infamous for brazenly supervising rigging, violence and unrivalled abuse of state monopoly of violence in 2007. One of the remaining cases from this brigandage is that of the tribunal considering the petition for confirming the popular mandate given to us by the people of Osun state.

In our demand for the vote of the Osun electorate, we promised PEOPLE FRIENDLY GOVERNANCE and a serving leadership. We posited HUMANISM as the core solution to most socio-economic and political problems currently overwhelming the majority of Nigerians. Our special concerns are however for the people of Osun State where over sixty percent of the populations are under forty years of age in a basically agrarian subsistence economy.

In developing this thesis, we arqued that democracy as practised today is highly flawed. But we also acknowledged the Churchillian dictum that whatever the flaw in democracy, no better political system has yet been devised to ensure justice and LIFE MORE ABUNDANT TO ALL.

We however agree that we must revert to the basic hypothesis of President Abraham Lincoln, that political activity like life, is about people. We must also admit that the human animal is as of right ENTITLED to a good life through a political system in which he/she can best fulfill his/her human dignity, one that promises to him/her and remains FRIENDLY to him/her.

In the circumstance, we would like to suggest that while democracy as practiced today remains the most effective and efficient system for the participation of all in all communities, a way has to be found, new and original mechanisms designed, to ensure that political life is and remains FRIENDLY to the people in all communities. To our mind people friendly governance will most definitely sanitize the theory and practice of democracy.

So we must ask what PFG (People Friendly Governance) means? To answer this question correctly we need to disabuse many minds of the notion that all systems of the modern age, socio-economic and political in particular, are solely products of the Western intellectual tradition. It is also so easy to succumb to the "illusion of technology" and to the arrogance and hubris of the German Sociologist' Max Weber who in his classic study of 'the Protestant Ethics and the spirit of capitalism 'on p 13 of the Authony Giddens' edition, used the opening clause "ONLY IN THE WEST" do science, historical scholarship, Art, Architecture, the organization of trained officials (bureaucracy) the state, and capitalism itself exist in the sense and manner we have come to know it in the modern era, an epoch in which the rampaging civilization of Western Europe collided with those of Africa, Asia and the Americas overwhelming the latter to create the modern world in its own image. When and at the time this collision of cultures touched our narrow corridor of the Southern Atlantic the Yoruba with their own theory of creation had evolved a complex cultural system without the benefit of the three great Chinese inventions -Paper, Gun Powder and the Compass - inventions which fuelled the Western mind and exploded its genius.

In the Southwestern corner of what is today's Nigeria 'the Yoruba had created IFA as a knowledge system for managing the human condition for the benefit and advantage of the individual and the community. Their social and political organizations were advanced; their textile technology included the production of silk at a time Europe imported silk from the Orient. They created a food technology and agricultural system and culture that sustained a good quality of life to millions of their people. They paraded works of art, of unique creativity including the lost wax process etc. They established an intricate socio-political system and a constitutional monarchy which antedates the failed European experience where over ninety percent of the monarchies are extinct.

The Yoruba political system was based on the humanist philosophy of nurturing the dignity in all human beings (ONA LO JIN, ERU NI BABA). It enjoined assimilation and good treatment of aliens who were in Yoruba society allowed to participate in the political life of the community. The system recognises the right to a good life for all and CONSIDERS FAILURE IN ANY OF THESE A TRAGEDY.

Fifty years after political independence from the British colonizer, almost one hundred and fifty years since the first political act of foreign control over the Yoruba political space and almost seven hundred years since our world and culture collided with Europe's, WE THE YORUBA ARE IN A DOLDRUM.

Yoruba political life has become one of estrangement from our realities; of alienation from the modern world. We have become victims of socio-economic immobilism, fear, insecurity and an uncertain future for us, our children, our nation and the Nigerian state whose membership was imposed on us. In the context of this unprecedented psycho cultural damage & trauma, the Yoruba are crying for another Oduduwa to lead them, another Awolowo to restore them to the path of development and prosperity, a guide, leader and saviour, to free us from the tyranny of hegemonism. We are anxious to be part of a great experiment to lift us out of the dungeon on poverty, want and deprivation.

As the modern era matures, globalism only oppresses the poor, but Africa even more than colonialist exploitation. Western Europe and North America (WENA) mature into postmodernism. ASIA secures a foothold on the platform of the modern era, struggling and seriously handicapped by its large population. Africa remains in active prostration, surviving on cast-off political systems, consumer goods, deprivation and the agony of want in the presence of plenty- Africa's want, WENA's plenty.

Yes the Yoruba, guided by the core ethical stand on OMOLUWABI- (integrity and honor in life) remain traumatized by the failure of democracy to deliver them into the modern era which they desire and which they believe is their birth right. This sad and painful individual and group experience has rendered their ethical heritage untenable. Many of them have joined the Nigeria locust army and barbarians. Their Honor has been defaced, their Integrity maimed and the land of Omoluwabi desecrated.

Today's youth among the Yoruba- the unemployed educated, the underemployed pool of artisans, the Okada operators in hidden unemployment our frustrated and desiccated peasantry- are knowledgeable enough to know that the present political life to which they are chained is HELL ON EARTH. They also know what they NEED to make them more competitive, arm them with the capacity to match and/or surpass their counterparts in the rest of the world.

- They want to restructure the Nigerian State.
- They want regional autonomy.
- They want the rule of law.
- They want their human dignity back.
- They want to enjoy the fruits of their labor in peace.
- They want freedom from hunger, social insecurity and political Oppression.
- They wish to be lifted out of the doldrums.
- They also know that political life to be good, must deliver to them; PEOPLE FRIENDLY GOVERNANCE.

DECLARATION

It is the acknowledgment of these birthrights and the moral duty to organize, deliver and defend them that is the philosophical imperative of PEOPLE FRIENDLY GOVERNANCE- The operational principles are the firing of the urge, the rational organization of societies, peoples and communities to ensure that political life and space make possible the following:

(a) Substainable food security

(b) Full employment for youth and all persons of working age

(c) Creative Education and the provision of modern skills capacity

(d) Modern health care delivery system

(e) Prosperity in our time

(f) Peace and general progress for all.

Human dignity and a good life are not possible in the absence of the above and the above are the birthright of all human beings. It is also the bounden duty of all governments to ensure and deliver them. It is the duty of all to demand and defend them. It is only the individual working in groups that can compel adherence to PEOPLE FRIENDLY GOVERNANCE.

In Osun today as we cry aloud for the justice of the tribunal, we here in IROGBO call for the early institution of people friendly governance amongst us and promise this to our folks, young and old, men/women. We commit and will dedicate ourselves, lead our people to the life of political duty, obligations and responsibilities to ourselves and posterity.

This we shall demand, work for and defend as our birth right, that government in Nigeria be decolonized and repositioned as an agency for serving the people and for preserving human dignity. These and nothing else we can and should enshrine as the new order which will bring a new way of life- the path to honor and integrity - the way of the OMOLUWABI.

Let us go from Irogbo here to regain and refurbish the political space. Let us offer a political life which will be friendly enough to all our people, restore to them their dignity and deliver to them unconditionally:

FOOD SECURITY

THE DIGNITY OF COMMENSURATE RETURNS TO EFFORT/WORK

ENLIGHTMENT AND CREATIVITY

GOOD HEALTH AND LONG LIFE

ASCERTAINED PROSPERITY

PEACE AND PROGRESS

Osun state shall be our platform for change, our laboratory for demonstrating the viability of people friendly governance. From Irogbo to Osogbo we shall march and free our people from poverty and restore to them their dignity. ODUDUWA A GBE WA O.

05-05-2010

APPENDIX II

AIDE MEMOIRE and guidance notes on the philosophy/essence and purpose of Osun state OYES CADET VOLUNTEERS scheme

1) OYES is a revolving volunteers scheme designed to eliminate the frustration and paralyzing effect of unacceptably high and seemingly intractable youth unemployment pervasive in Osun nay, Nigeria .

It aims at creating a bridge to employment by equipping as many young men and women ; our new youth, with positive work ethics and culture, self sustenance, resourcefulness and respect for the environment. It is designed to develop youths with Character and Competence (the 2 Cs) – infusing them with HONOUR AND INTEGRITY IN LIFE....the virtues of an Omoluwabi

2) The OYES corps are deployed to productive services in identified areas of socio-economic life and paid a basic allowance to help cover basic needs. They are also smartly kitted for group identity and high morale.

3) In the past year, OYES cadets have performed extremely well on communal, social, economic and environmental projects of importance to the general public and have become an enviable marker for youth espirit de corps and can be proud of their presence in the community.

4) At the same time public reaction to their emergence, presence and activity in the community has been exceedingly positive.

5) In sharpening and heightening their civic responsibility in general and work ethics in particular, membership in the scheme has given the OYES corps members clear advantages in the general economy facilitating their attractiveness, suitability and in many cases recruitment into the civil service, agencies of government, private organisations who are partnering with the state government on the scheme, private sector employers, and patronage by government of their products and services.

6) Successful participation in the scheme is a unique opportunity for most corps members to acquire correct life attitudes, self confidence and improved skills within one year on the scheme.

7) The scheme could only accommodate 8% of those who applied as clearly shown below. When the OYES scheme was advertised, the enormity and size of skilled and graduate youth unemployment was revealed:

a. Over 250,000 youths applied to join the OsunYouth Empowerment Scheme (OYES) as Cadet Volunteers in December 2010. Majority of these were high school and tertiary institution graduates who had not found work eight to ten years after graduation
b. Of this quarter of a million applicants, about 200,000 were qualified to serve as Cadet Volunteers but the scheme is meant for 20,000.
c. As promised in the PACT with the people of Osun State, 20,000 persons were recruited as the first batch of the OYES in fulfillment of Governor Aregbesola's promise to engage 20,000 persons within his first 100 days in office.
d. A responsible People Friendly Government (PFG) cannot ignore such a large and growing pool of qualified and competent youth desirous of some form of engagement to improve their lives. That is why the scheme must be a rolling and not static scheme.

In so doing your government would at the end of the day have turned almost a quarter of a million previously stagnating, frustrated and confused young men and women into good quality, highly motivated citizens, who are work ready and exceptionally competitive for the Nigerian economy and society.

e. In the above context, the win-win, is the robust exit strategy that has been put in place to facilitate the entrance of the first batch into the Nigerian economy, by improving their capacity, empowering them and virtually ensuring that they can better walk into life- long careers.

As part of the exit strategy, they shall be armed with new skills, entrepreneurship and mentoring as part of efforts of the government of the State of Osun to prepare them for honourable and gainful exit from the scheme.

f. This would create a healthy flow into the state and national economies and at the same time allow another batch of 20,000 still unemployed youths to experience the benefits of serving as Cadet Volunteers in OYES,.
g. At OYES, a family culture is emerging which will enable graduating volunteers to remain part of the scheme as proud alumni and ambassadors for OYES after meritoriously being stamped as cadets of a corps designed to shape character and infuse competence...our 2Cs for their lives ....GEGE BI OMOLUWABI

APPENDIX III

OYES OSUN YOUTH EMPOWERMENT SCHEME

(A VOLUNTEER PROGRAMME)

APPLICATION FORM ……

Please complete this form accurately, giving as many details as possible of your skills and experience. Short listing will be based on the information gathered from this form

GUIDELINES

Please ensure the finished form is signed, thumb printed, dated and returned to the address indicated on the last page

Please complete the form in black ink and BLOCK CAPITALS

1. PERSONAL INFORMATION

Title:	*Surname*	*First name:*	*Middle Name*	*Sex*

Residential address:	*No of years at this address*

Date of Birth	*Place of Birth:*	*State of Origin*	*Local Government Area*

Religion	*Marital Status:*	*Spouse Full name:*	*No of Children*

Telephone Nos:
email address (*where possible*):

Identification			
Do you hold a valid driver's licence?	Yes/No	**Driver's Licence No**	

Do you hold a National ID card?	Yes/No	**Nationl ID No**	

Any other form of identification	Yes/No	**Type/Detail**	

Medical Records:	
If you have a disability which requires reasonable adjustments at the selection interview, or which needs to be taken into account when considering your application please let us know. Reasonable adjustments would include sign language interpreters, altering the time of the interview or making the interview room accessible for you	
Physical Disability: *[tick as appropriate]*	***Allergy or medical reactions***
☐ No Disability ☐ Ear ☐ Eyes	☐ No Allergy/medical reaction
☐ Hand ☐ Leg ☐ Other ________	☐ Specify ________________

2. EMPLOYMENT RECORD

Please state your most recent employment/Experience.

1. Current/most recent employer/organisation				
Name:				
Address:				
Job Title:	From:		To:	
Brief description of duties:				
Reason for leaving/changing:				

2. Employer/organisation				
Name:				
Address:				
Job Title:	From:		To:	
Brief description of duties:				
Reason for leaving/changing:				

3. EDUCATION			
Please tell us about your education and any qualifications obtained. Include relevant courses which you are currently undertaking. Please start with the most recent.			
Name of school/college/ university/training body	*Subject studied*	*Qualification / Level*	*Date Obtained*

4. TRAINING	
Please list any training /vocation or experience you have received, or courses which did not lead to a qualification but which may be relevant to a job application. Please attach relevant evidence	
Training Course	*Date*

5. EXPERIENCE / SKILLS
Please state how you want to contribute to the positive development of Osun state through the Osun Youth Corps

6. JOB INTEREST		
This section is for you to list, in order of importance, the job types that suit your interest as well as your preferred job location		
Preferred job type in order of importance	*Preferred job location in order of importance*	*Reason for location preference*
1.		
2.		
3.		
Preferred Job arrangement [Tick as appropriate]		
☐ No Preference	☐ Environmental Sanitation	☐ Traffic control
☐ Agriculture	☐ Road maintenance	☐ Tree Planting/ Horticulture
☐ Others – please specify		

7. REFERENCES	
Please give name, address and position/occupation of two referees.	
1. Name:	
Position:	
Organisation:	
Address:	
Tel:	Relationship :

2. Name:	
Position:	
Organisation:	
Address:	
Tel:	Relationship :

8. DECLARATION AND SIGNATURE

I certify that my answers are true and complete to the best of my knowledge. If this application leads to employment, I understand that false or misleading information in my application or interview may result in my disqualification.

Signed Thumbprint Date

Thank you for completing the form. Please Return Completed form to your Local Government

THIS FORM IS FREE

APPENDIX IV

NAME: ....
OYES NO: ....
DATE: ....

THE OSUN YOUTH EMPOWERMENT SCHEME (OYES)
LETTER OF ENGAGEMENT AS A VOLUNTEER CADET

Following your successful application, selection and completion of the mandatory training course prescribed for Osun Youth Empowerment Scheme (hereinafter referred to as OYES)Volunteer Cadet, the OYES Secretariat is pleased to inform you of your engagement as a member of OYES Volunteer Cadet subject to the terms and conditions herein provided.

TERMS OF MEMBERSHIP

1. Your membership as an OYES Volunteer Cadet takes effect from 1st of July 2012, and shall be for a period of two years.
2. Your membership of the OYES Volunteer Cadet will entitled you to a monthly stipend of **N10,000.00 (Ten Thousand Naira Only)** effect from the date of engagement.
3. Your membership of the OYES Volunteer Cadet is not an employment in the civil/public service of the State of Osun and do not entitle you to the remunerations and any other entitlements of members of the State of Osun Civil/Public Service. Further, your membership of the OYES Volunteer Cadet is not pensionable.
4. In keeping with the Volunteer Cadet's Code of Conduct, (as in the Cadet's Training Manual) you shall carry out your assigned lawful duties with a high sense of responsibility, moral soundness, probity and total commitment, in accordance with the virtues of **Omoluabi**, an honourable person.
5. The value of **Omoluabi** comprising honesty, integrity, hard work, discipline, safety, competence, respect for all, oneness, leadership and loyalty shall also be your watchword and you shall abide and comply with same.

6. You shall comply with the rules set out in the **OYES Cadet's Code of Conduct** which is deemed to be part of this letter. Disciplinary procedures shall be exercised with regards to any violations of the said Code of Conduct.
7. The OYES Secretariat reserves the right to deploy you to any part of the State, Country or internationally and assign you to any developmental project, task or services as may be determined by the appropriate organs of OYES.
8. You shall exhibit sense of discipline and responsibility at all times and your membership may be summarily terminated for breach of discipline or failure to obey lawful instructions.
9. Without prejudice to the right of the OYES Secretariat to terminate your membership engagement summarily on disciplinary ground, your membership engagement may be terminated voluntarily by one month notice or payment of one month stipend in lieu of notice.
10. In all cases of termination, you shall return all properties of OYES in your possession/custody including, but not limited to, your uniform and kits to the OYES secretariat in a decent and usable state.

This offer of Volunteer cadet membership is provisional and shall become valid only upon receipt of a written letter of acceptance of offer in your own hand written within 7 working days of receipt of this letter.

Congratulations

Col EniIbukun Oyewole (rtd)
Commandante

APPENDIX V

INTERVIEW WITH MRS ADEDEJI IDOWU, A FORMER OYES CADET

SADE ADEWALE - LAWAL

Sade: E kaasan ma

Adedeji: E kaasan

Sade: Oruko mi ni iyaafin Adewale-Lawal. Mo wa s'oju fun Dokita Ajewumi Raji ti Obafemi Awolowo University lati wa bayin soro nipa OYES. E je ka bere nipa alaye die nipa ara yin

Adedeji: Oruko mi ni Adedeji Idowu. Mo wa lati Osogbo local government. Mo je okan lara OYES cadet first batch. Ni aarin igba ti a se OYES yen, akoko, nigba ti a bere ise yen bi ana,ti a ko mope rere naa ni o ma ja si. Nigba ti a bere ise yen, won ni a ma maa gbale ni esese titi, ki a ma gba awon idoti ti o wa ni ese titi, won de nsan owo fun wa ni osoosu. Won nsan 10,000 fun wa ni osoosu. Ti o ba di ipari odun, won tun ma fun wa ni bonus 13th month ni December. So nigba ti a nse ise yen lo, awon anfani kookan wa nibe ti o je wipe won introduce si wa

Sade: Bawo ni e se ro nigba ti wonni ki e ma ma gba idoti egbe titi?e ro wipe odidi eyin a kuro ni'le yin lati ma gba idoti kiri. Bawo ni e se ri si nigbayen?

Adedeji: A koko ro pe egbe titi bawo. Sugbon nigba ti a de ibe, a ri wipe awon kan ma wa ti won fe ma gba ile yi gan, bi o tie je pe #500 ni awon o ma gba gan. Ti o je wipe ki anfani yi tie yo fun won, ni awa wa ri ni ofe lofo, bi gbogbo wa se be mo niyen la ba bere si ni je anfani yen lo diedie. Nigba ti a bere si ni je anfani e, a mo wipe nkankan tun wa labe ile gbigba yi ti o ju ile gbigba yi lo. Lara awon nkan ti o wa labe pe a gba ile yii nipe, won introduce awon programme kookan ti a pe ni exit programme si wa nigba yen. Lara awon exit programme yen ni O'reap wa, lara e ni Odua Farm Settlement wa. Lara e ni won ti ko wa ni liquid soap ati disinfectant tiemi nje anfani e loni, ti mo fi nse ise se lowolowo bayi

Sade: E ko mo nipa e rara tele, ki won to ko yin?

Adedeji: Mi o mo nipa e rara tele. Ninu OYES ni mo ti ko. Ohun ni mo de nfi se ise se loni, ti mo joko ti, ti mo nje loni. Mi o ni ise mi leyin re ti mo nje. Liquid wash yen ati disinfectant ohun ni mon se. die lara awon liquid wash yen, being pe mo fe travel, mi o ni production nile bayi, sugbon mo ni liquid wash nile,mo de ni awon disinfectant ti mi o ti ro. O si wa ninu jerry can. Then lara awon disinfectant yen, awon kan wa ni OYES office to je wipe ti e ba de ibe e ma ri OYES disinfectant ni ara re, ti o je wipe emi ni mo se. ti o de je wipe won nta nibe. Nibeyen, mo tun nri owo. OYES office gangan ni white house, o wa nibe lowolowo bi mo se nsoro yi. Phone number mi wa lara e. Emi ti mo se naa niyi

Sade: Se OYES office ti ibi ti awon eeyan ma npe ni Aregbesola?

Adedeji: Beeni, ibe lo wa. So, t'eyan ba de ibe, e o ba nibe. Mo de tun nko awon eeyan bi won se nse liquid wash yen, sugbon emi o ni ibi Kankan ti mo ti ko. Inu OYES yen ni mo ti je anfani yen. Ti o je wipe kii se pe won ni kin mu owo wa ki nwa fi ko tabi kin mu obi wa. Nigba yen lohun ti won ni ki a wa ko, won mu eeyan mejimeji ni local government kookan. A de ni 31 local governments ni Osun state nigbayen. Thirty one local governments yen, won mu eeyan mejimeji. Mo je okan lara awon eeyan meji ti won mu ni Osogbo local government nigbayen. So, lara awon ti won mu nigbayen ti won ni ki a wa se oriire, ki won wa je anfani ekose yen, emi je enikan ti mo nfi se ise se lowolowo bayi, ti mo fi njeun loni, to je wipe mi o ni nkan miran pelu e

Sade: E se ma. E se training kan ki o to di wipe won deploy yin lo si ibi ti e ti ma se ise.o dabi eni wipe ose meta nigbayen, ti won ti ko yin ni orisirisi nkan.mo gbo wipe nigba ti e pari nigbayen, won fun yin lowo fun training?

Adedeji: Igba ti a sese bere OYES yen, a se training ni St. Charles ti o je wipe awon military ni won train wa. A ma nlo si parade yen nigbayen. Nigba ti a se training yen, won fun wa ni awon aso ti a fi se, ti o je wipe ofe ni won fun wa, lai gba owo. Leyin igba ti a pari training yen, won tun fun wa ni owo'training allowance'. Leyin igba ti won fun wa ni training allowance yen, won tun wa fun wa ni uniform ti a ma ma wo lati fi se ise ni ofe, lai gba owo lowo enikankan ninu wa

Sade: Yato si exit programme ti e ti ko nipa ose yi, ibo ni won deploy yin si nigba ti e pari training?

Adedeji: igba ti mo pari training, sanitation ni won deploy mi si

Sade: Ok ma

Adedeji: Nigba ti a nse sanitation yen lo, won tun wa se another deployment. Mo fall si road maintenance nigbayen. So nigba ti a nse road maintenance yen, ti koriko ma wu legbe titi a o san. Nitori eni tio je oga wa nigbayen ma nba wa da asa kan pe "in military we are all men" pe ati okunrin, ati obinrin o. okunrin ni wa. So, ko si nkan ti okunrin le se ti obinrin o le se. nigbayen won fi wa si egbegbe titi pe ti oko ba ti nkun, ki a ma san tabi ki a ro. Ti a ba ro, a o gba, a je ki gbogbo ibe ki o neat. Won so wipe, igbe lowo wa, ninu ibi ti a tin se awon ise diedie bayi, ibe naa ni anfani nkan ti mo nje loni ti jade

Sade: Oluwa seun.igba ti mo pe yin pemo mbo, e so wipe e ni lati se nkankan pelu awon OYES ni eni. Ki ni nkan ti e fe lo se fun won yen? Se o ni se pelu ise ti e nse?

Adedeji: Beeni. Nigba ti e pe mi pe e mbo yen, mo ti ni programme pelu awon OYES cadet kan ti mo fe ko bi won se nse liquid wash ati disinfectant yen. Ti o je wipe emi lo ye kin lo. Sugbon nigba ti o je wipe emi atiyin o ri'ra ri, openi lo de nsola, mo ni lati koko je ipe yin

Sade: E se ma. Se awon OYES cadet ti e fe se training fun yen, se eyin le yan won? Abi won wa ba yin funra won? Abi awon ara Osogbo local government yin ni e fe se fun?

Adedeji: Gbogbo local government ni mo ma nse fun. Gbogbo local government ti o wa ni Osun state ni mo ma nse fun. Mo ti se fun awon Irewole, mo ti se fun won ni Ife north, mo ti se fun won ni Orolu, ti o je wipe mo train won. Mo ti train awon kan naa ni Osogbo, Olorunda ti o je wipe won ti mo nipa ise yi

Sade: Tani o ma nsan owo training fun yin? Se awon cadet naa ni abi ijoba?

Adedeji: Awon cadet ki I san owo. Ofe ni won ma nko?

Sade: Se ofe ni eyin ma nko won? E ki I gba nkankan?

Adedeji: Beeni. Leyin ti won ba ti ra materials, ti won ti ra chemical, a ki I gba owo lowo won. Nitori ijoba ipinle Osun ti won ko wan naa, ofe ni won ko wa

Sade: Se awon ni won pe yin pe ki e wa ma se fun won abi eyin le volunteer lati ma se fun won ni oorekoore?

Adedeji: Eni to je oga wa patapata Commandante, Eniibukun Oyewole, awon ni won pe mi pe ninu anfani ti emi naa je, nigba ti emi naan se OYES, pe kin fun awon to si wa nibe ni die ninu e. ki awon naa le je anfani yen

Sade: Ti won ba wa ni pe ki e gba ijoba ni imoran lori oro OYES lati te siwaju, tabi akiyesi yin nibi ti o ku die kaato, ti e le ro pe o ye ki won se daadaa ju be lo, kini awon nkan ti e ma so fun wa?

Adedeji: Nkan ti mo kan ri nipa OYES cadet nipe, o daa bi won se nro awon odo lagbara, sugbon, ibi to ku die nipe, nkan ti awa nse jade, ti o je wipe, ogbeni naa lo kun wa lowo de'be ti a fi le ni anfani ati se nkan yen, boya ti a ba le gbe awon nkan yi laruge, boya o le ma pa owo wole fun wa ni ipinle Osun

Sade: Bii?

Adedeji: Bi disinfectant yen, ti won ba le je ki a ma se, ki a ma ko si awon hopitals wa, awon maternity centre. Ohun naa ni won kun lo. Awon eeyan naa lo nse eyi ti won ngbaruku ti yen ti won nlo. So ti won ba le gbaruku ti eleyi ti o je wipe awa naa la nse, boya yoo ma pa owo wole fun wa ni ipinle Osun

Sade: Yato si disinfectant ati liquid wash yi, awon nkan wo lo tun je ise owo tabi elo ile ti won tun ko awon mii, boya ti awon elomii tun ko?

Adedeji: A tun ma nse air freshner, a ma nse bleach, mon se bleach. O wa lara awon nkan ti a se. nigba ti a se passing out parade wa nigbayen, nigba ti a pari, ti a fe kuro, ninu awon packaging ti o je wipe ogbeni Aregbesola gangan, won ra 22 packs fun awon lobaloba ipinle Osun ti won wa si parade yen nijoyen, ti mo de wa nibe. Oga wa patapata, iyen Col. Eniibukun Oyewole niwon mu won wa si ibi ti a wa, lati wa ra awon oja yen nigbayen. Won ra fun gbogbo awon lobaloba ti won wa, pack Kankan bi a se pack e. Disinfectant, liquid soap ati bleach ni o wa ninu pack yen

Sade: E se a dupe ma. Inu mi dun pe e fun wa ni anfani lati ba yin soro ni osan yi. E se, Olorun a ma ran yin lowo. Ise yin naa a si ma a gbooro lagbara Olorun. E se.

TRANSLATION

Sade: Good afternoon ma

Adedeji: Good afternoon

Sade: My name is Mrs. Adewale-Lawal. I am here representing Dr. Ajewumi Raji of Obafemi Awolowo University, Ile-Ife. I am here to interview you on OYES. Let's start with a brief introduction about yourself

Adedeji: My name is Adedeji Idowu. I am from Osogbo local government. I was one of the 1st batch of OYES cadets. Everything seems like yesterday, when we started the work, we never knew it will turn out to be this rewarding. We were told that we will be sweeping the road sides, and we were paid monthly for this. We were being paid 10,000 monthly. In addition to this, at the end of the year, we were given 13th month salary in December. So when we were doing this work, some other benefits were later introduced to us.

Sade: How did you feel when you were told that you will be sweeping the road sides? Don't you think the assignment was derogatory to your person? What did you think about it?

Adedeji: Initially we didn't feel good about it, but when we got there, we realized that there are a lot of people out there who desire the opportunity to do such work even at a monthly pay of 5,000, but could not get it. With that thought, we saw it as an opportunity and we embraced it. When we started the work, we never knew there were some other hidden benefits. Part of the hidden benefit is the exit programme which was later introduced to us. The exit programme includes, O'reap, Odua farm settlement and training on how to make liquid soap and disinfectant which I do today as a source of livelihood.

Sade: You knew nothing about it before you were taught?

Adedeji: I knew nothing about it before then. I learnt about it from OYES, and that is what I'm feeding on today. I have just a little production on ground now, because I am travelling. If not, I normally produce it in large quantity. The disinfectant I produce, labelled "OYES disinfectant" is sold at OYES office. That gives me additional money. My phone number is on the label which indicates that I produce it. It is presently at the white house.

Sade: Do you mean the OYES office where people refer to as Aregbesola?

Adedeji: Yes. That is where my disinfectant is being sold. I also train people on how to produce the liquid soap. I never had the fore knowledge, I learnt it from OYES without paying a dime for the training. When the training was introduced to us, two people were chosen from each local government, and we had thirty one local governments in Osun state then. I was one of the two people chosen from Osogbo local government. So, out of all of us chosen for the training then, I am one of those who live by the training today. I do not have any other source of income apart from this.

Sade: Thank you ma. You underwent training before you were deployed to your area of primary assignment. I learnt you were also paid for that. Is that true?

Adedeji: When we started OYES then, we did the training at St Charles, and we were trained by the military and we go on parade then. We were given uniform for the training, free of charge, and after the training, we were also given training allowance. Afterwards, they also gave us uniform for our primary assignment. All these were given to us at no cost at all.

Sade: Apart from the Exit programme where you learn how to make liquid soap, where were you deployed after the training?

Adedeji: After the training, I was deployed to sanitation

Sade: Ok ma

Adedeji: While we were deployed to sanitation, they did another deployment and I fell under road maintenance. We cut grasses by the road side. Our boss then has a saying that "in military we are all men" meaning that -what a man can do, a woman can also do. We were positioned by the road side, to cut the grass and sweep. We were to ensure that everywhere is neat. It is where we were doing all these that I had additional benefit of what I feed on today.

Sade: Thank God. When I called you, you told me that you needed to do something with the OYES cadet. Does what you want to do have to do with your work?

Adedeji: Yes. When you called me, I already have an appointment with some cadets. I wanted to teach them how to make liquid soap and disinfectant. But when you called me, I have to honour you because we have not met before.

Sade: Thank you ma. Did you choose those OYES cadets you wanted to train by yourself? Or they came to meet you on their own? Or they are from your local government, Osogbo local government?

Adedeji: I do the training for all the local government in Osun state. I have done it for Irewole local government, I have done at Ife North, I have also trained some people at Orolu local government. Also, I have trained some people in Osogbo and Olorunda local government as well.

Sade: Who normally pays you for these trainings? Is it the cadets or the government?

Adedeji: The cadets do not pay. I train them free of charge

Sade: Do you train them for free, without collecting a dime?

Adedeji: All they do is to buy the materials by themselves. When they buy the chemicals, I train them for free because Osun state government also trained me for free.

Sade: Were you called by the government to give the training or you volunteered to do so at regular intervals?

Adedeji: I was invited by our overall boss, commandante, in person of Col. Eniibukun Oyewole (Rtd). He said I should impart the knowledge I acquired from the exit programme, which is the making of liquid soap and disinfectant into other cadets.

Sade: If you are to advise the government on OYES, probably in areas of improvement or observations, what would you say?

Adedeji: What I just want to say about OYES is that, it is good as the youths are being empowered, but if the government can uplift our locally made products which we even acquire the training through them, it may be a good source of income for the government

Sade: Like?

Adedeji: The disinfectant for instance can be taken to hospitals and maternity homes. Undoubtedly, that is what they even use in those hospitals and maternity homes. But if we can introduce ours, it could be another source of income generation for Osun state government

Sade: Apart from this disinfectant and liquid wash, what are other skills or home use products that people were trained for?

Adedeji: We also make air freshener and bleach. I make bleach. It is one of our products for the passing out parade then. In fact, Ogbeni Rauf Aregbesola bought 22packs of our products and gave to the kings that were present at the passing out. It was Col. Eniibukun Oyewole who brought the governor to patronize us. He bought for all the Osun state monarchs who were present at the occasion. Each pack contained, disinfectant, liquid soap and bleach

Sade: Thank you so much ma. I am glad that you gave me the opportunity to speak with you this afternoon. May your work continue to prosper. Thank you.

APPENDIX VI

INTERVIEW WITH MR. IBRAHIM JAMIU (CONDUCTED ON 1ST DEC, 2016).

SADE ADEWALE - LAWAL

Sade: Hello good afternoon. My name is Mrs FolasadeAdewale-Lawal. I'm here representing Dr. Raji of Obafemi Awolowo University. I am here to conduct an interview with you regarding OYES. So let me just start by asking you to give me a background information about yourself

Jamiu: Thank you so much. I am Ibrahim Jamiu. I am a native of Osogbo. I was born and brought up in Osogbo town. I'm a boy, I'm not a man

Sade: Boy? Why did you say that?

Jamiu: Because a man is somebody that has the capacity to handle big family affairs.

Sade: That is your own interpretation of man?

Jamiu: Yes

Sade: So you are not yet a family man?

Jamiu: I'm a family man. Not the standard one, but a small one

Sade: You have a wife and kids, and you still call yourself a boy?

Jamiu: Yes, I'm a boy

Sade: Then what do we call your little boy at home?

Jamiu: A boy too

Sade: You are a man. So, let's proceed please

Jamiu: I have a National Diploma in mass communication, and I joined OYES in 2011. Precisely March, 2011

Sade: Is that the first batch?

Jamiu: Yes, first batch. So our batch ended in 2013, but before we completed our tenure then, I was already attached to our commander general, in person of Col. Eniibukun Oyewole

Sade: So before you finished your tenure then, you were...

Jamiu: Appointed as media assistant to the commandant of OYES

Sade: why were you appointed among every other cadets there?

Jamiu: Because I was a journalist who specializes in photo journalism before I joined OYES. The commandante needed a photo journalist then and that was why I was appointed to work with him.

Sade: What do you do for him?

Jamiu: I take pictures of events for him and also when need be

Sade: Before you found yourself in OYES, have you worked with any media before? Either print or broadcast?

Jamiu: Yes and no. before I joined OYES, I am a graphic editor. I have been editing for daily post newspaper, assisting Mr. Komolafe Olorunnisola. Komolafe Olorunnisola is the chief editor while I was assisting him in editing photography then. That was between 2010 and 2011

Sade: Let's go back to OYES. Can you please tell me what your training in OYES entails? Before you were deployed, were you actually deployed into photography? Is there even anything like photoghaphy in OYES?

Jamiu: I was deployed into sanitation

Sade: That is what everyone does

Jamiu: Firstly when you engage in OYES, before you will be deployed, you will firstly go into sanitation for six months

Sade: Six months?

Jamiu: Yes six months. During that time, I was called that Commandante will like to see me. When I got to him he asked if I have a digital camera. I said Yes. He asked further "how much did you get the camera for?" I told him #58,000. He also asked me how I got the money to buy the camera. I now explained to him that, before the inception of OYES, I had a practical digital camera which I bought for #8,000

Sade: #8,000?

Jamiu: Yes #8,000. He checked my name on the list. The following day I resumed to the training camp where I was taking shots of cadets during the training before the class section. Then I printed the pictures and gave them to the cadets. Within that three weeks, I realized more than #50,000. I added another #10,000 that I had on me to the money I realized and used it to buy the camera. I used the camera for Commandante between 2011 and 2012 before I bought another camera

Sade: But by the time you were attending to fellow cadets at the training, were you able to do what you were supposed to do at the training?

Jamiu: Yes, because I had a platoon. Even my commandant in that platoon accepted it as a good idea. He said I should make sure I see him anytime I'm through with my business.

Sade: Does that mean you gave him a share of the money you realized?

Jamiu: No. it was just a joke.

Sade: That means you did not learn anything about photography in OYES?

Jamiu: I didn't but I had additional training when I got to OYES.

Sade: Were people trained for photography in OYES?

Jamiu: Yes. I usually excused myself at weekends then, I tell them I have functions where I will do the video coverage and photography. It was then that my boss told me that I can actually train OYES cadets in photography. But I told him I do not have the license to do it. I introduced Mr. Odekayo to come and train them. We have an institute of photography. I invited them to come and train the OYES cadets. Up till now, we have trained about 320 cadets in photography.

Sade: As an exit programme ?

Jamiu: Yes, as an exit programme. Farming is also an exit programme in OYES. You can partake in any skill of your choice as an exit programme in OYES. If you do not like farming, you can go for bead making. You can go for cake making, even photography.

Sade: It all depends on what each person wants then?

Jamiu: Yes. You can also decide not to partake in any of the exit programmes. It is your choice. You cannot be forced on that, you can only be advised.

Sade: What are the benefits you have derived so far on OYES?

Jamiu: Personal benefit, when I joined OYES I was a secondary school certificate holder in 2011, but now I can boldly say that I am an ND holder

Sade: So, you started your ND after joining OYES?

Jamiu: Yes, when I joined OYES. That is in education line.

Sade: Ok

Jamiu: Secondly,

Sade: Sorry, that your ND, you started it when you joined OYES?

Jamiu: Yes. I applied to OYES with a secondary school certificate. When I got to OYES, through my income, I started my ND and I completed it. Secondly, it was when I got to OYES that I bought a piece of land and built a house on it. So I live in my own house now. The first camera I bought was in OYES and I bought it for 58,000 naira. Now, I have a camera of 320,000, 240,000 and 529,000

Sade: Everything from OYES?

Jamiu: Yes

Sade: What about your photography business during weekends?

Jamiu: Everything is from OYES because if I have not been involved in OYES, I might not have had the opportunity to do it

Sade: So we can say you got empowered in photography through OYES?

Jamiu: Yes

Sade: Ok. Thank you very much. So what is your overall view of OYES? Areas you want the government to improve on, your observation and any other thing you want to tell us about OYES

Jamiu: My observation, don't keep what you have to yourself. I forgot to tell you that, after school cert, I told my father to keep his money that I do not want to further my education again, that I wanted to learn photography

Sade: You wanted to strive on your own?

Jamiu: Yes. I told him that I wanted to go and learn photography. That he should not bother himself about my going to school. He said he will have to call a family meeting to let them know my decision so that they can bear him witness. I told him to permit me to learn photography, then I will further my education later. He should not just spend on me anymore. He accepted, and now he has never regretted granting my request.

Sade: You said you told your daddy that you wanted to learn photography, and you also said that it was when you got to OYES that you did your ND in mass communication and specialized in photography, does it mean you have been learning about it before coming to OYES?

Jamiu: Yes. OYES empowers me in photography. I have been learning it, but I could not afford to buy the equipment

Sade: But you said you were working with the daily post?

Jamiu: No, I was just the graphics editor

Sade: Before you got to OYES?

Jamiu: Yes. That was 2010 to 2011. I have learnt it between 2006 and 2009. I learnt photography and graphic design. So when I got appointment with daily post, I specialized in editing and packaging of the page. When I got to OYES, the first camera I bought, I borrowed #8,000 to buy the trash camera. So I later realized #58,000 from OYES to buy a digital camera which I used for my freedom in photography. I learnt it, but unable to do the freedom. It was when I got to OYES that I realized the money that I used to buy a professional camera needed for my freedom.

Sade: Ok. I was asking for areas that you think OYES could improve on, new ideas to make it better than the way it is now?

Jamiu: If I want to talk about new innovation, I will just be beating around the bush. I thank God for the life of Col. Eniibukun Oyewole (Rtd). If you start a programme, it is always good to get someone who can handle it properly, in order not to regret starting it. In 2012, Col. Eniibukun Oyewole designed an exit programme, he was concerned about personal empowerment of OYES cadets. Like a take home skill. As a cadet, you collect that #10,000 and use it to eat? No. you can save out of the #10,000 to buy freezer to sell frozen foods, you can sell recharge cards, and you can even buy fowls and establish yourself with a small amount. He now make it mandatory that as an OYES cadet, you must have another means of income apart from your salary. So we all went into different vocations. I even know of a lady, Olaosebikan from Ife East, he gathered #45,000 and travelled to Lagos for 2weeks training where she learnt how to use Ankara to sew shoes and bags. She can even use Ankara to make bouquet used by brides in weddings. When she came back from the training in Lagos, commandante asked me to interview her. If you have something in mind and you do not have someone to establish it for you, you cannot do it. It will just seem that you don't know what to do. In addition, Mr. Governor said that he wants to create another 20,000 cadets, what I will advise him is that, during the training, each cadet should specify his or her area of interest for the exit programme. Committee should be appointed to see to it, so that after the training, cadets can start the learning immediately

Sade: But I think the exit programme is a thing of choice and interest?

Jamiu: Yes. But it will be better if it is made compulsory for every cadet. You can decide you want to engage in a particular programme, while you have potential for another. You can be helped to discover your talent.

Sade: That means you think that you can decide for me?

Jamiu: Yes. I was once told to go into farming. I told the person that I do not know about it

Sade: Have you given it a trial?

Jamiu: In my compound now, I am a small farmer

Sade: That's good

Jamiu: That means that person must have seen something in me, which I didn't see. You can actually look at somebody and tell the person what to do

Sade: Does that mean you can actually study somebody and tell him the area where he can succeed?

Jamiu: Yes

Sade: I hope I will be welcome any other time

Jamiu: You are always welcome

Sade: Thank you very much. Do have a nice day

Jamiu: Thank you.

APPENDIX VII

INTERVIEW WITH MR. ISKILU BOLARINWA (CONDUCTED ON 24TH DECEMBER, 2016).

ADETOKUNBO ADEOLA SHITTU

AS: e jo'o, ma fe ki e introduce ara yin briefly

AS: I will like you to kindly introduce yourself briefly

BI: oruko temi ni Iskilu Bolarinwa, mo si je okan lara awon pioneer cadet members ni Osogbo Local Government. I am one of the prefects in Osogbo Local Government

BI: my name is Iskilu Bolarinwa, I am one of the pioneer members of the OYES in Osogbo Local Government. I am also one of the prefects in Osogbo Local Government

AS: bawo ni e se di eni to ko pa ninu eto OYES? Kini awon igbese to niise pelu bi e se ko'pa ninu eto OYES?

AS: how did you become a partaker of the OYES programme? What were the steps that were involved?

BI: akoko na, a gba form. Won issue form jade lati le mu ki a benefit ninu eto na. se e ri gbogbo nkan laye yi lo wa lowo kadara. Honestly, mo gba form yen late. Late form ni mo gba ni ojo to ma close ade try lati submit. At the end of the day, a submit won de paste oruko; Olorun de kadara pe ka je okan lara awon OYES members ti won choose. After igba yen won de pe gbogbo wa si training. After igba ti a se training- a se training yen boya bi a month plus- won deploy wa si Local Government a de carry out awon assignment wa ni iba yen. Won fun wa ni awon assignment community work; OYES is based on community work. From then a den attend different programmes to waye lori e. awon to wa impressed igba ti a n se community work wa won collaborate pelu OYES; awon ministries and organisations so pe awon maa need assistance OYES. Ti won ba de ti wa bayen, a ma lo se…a ma pe awon omoleyin wa…eyin naa e wa…e je ka jo se kini yi.

BI: firstly, I obtained a form. Some forms were issued out to enable us the youths benefit and take part in the programme. You see, all things in life have to do with destiny. I actually got the form late right on the closing date for submission. I managed to submit it and the names of successful applicants were later pasted. Afterwards, we were all invited for a training that lasted about a month or a little more, we were deployed to Local Governments to carry out assignments. We were assigned community works; OYES is all about community service. From then we attended different programmes that came up. Those organisations that got impressed by our works in the communities collaborated with OYES; ministries and organisations asked for our services. Each time they came, we obliged them and went with other junior cadet member to do the works assigned.

AS: e se mo dupe. Se e le daruko die fun wa lara awon eto to tun wa beneficial si awon OYES members ti won pe yin si?

AS: thank you so very much. Can you mention some of the beneficial programmes to which the OYES cadets were invited?

BI: boya, ti a o ba gbagbe, mo sir anti awon water corporation nigba yen, won collaborate pelu wa. Awon OWMA awon naa collaborate pelu wa but won need lati carry awon assignment kan fun wa. Then awon ministry of education won collaborate pelu wa. Igba yen ni won fe bere feeding, school feeding…

BI: I remember vividly our work with the water corporation. OWMA too collaborated with us by assigning us some duties. We also did some work for the Ministry of Education when they were about to start the school feeding programme.

AS: OMEAL?

BI: OMEAL. Ni igba yen a de carry out awon research wa. A carry out assignment yen. Awon ministry of education won collaborate pelu wa lati je ki a mo oye awon student ti o wa ni class kookan from primary 1-3 nigba yen. Awa la se programme yen

BI: OMEAL. Then we did a research to find out how many pupils were in each class from primary 1-3

AS: so, eyin le carry out research lati provide statistical data nipa awon pupils to wa ni school?

AS: so, it was the OYES cadets that researched to provide statistical data on the population of pupils in the schools?

BI: yes, ni primary school kookan. After result research ti a se, government de gbe igbese le lori. Won mo iye omo to wa ni schools kookan.

BI: yes, in each primary school. Government acted based on the outcome of our research. They could tell precisely the number of students being prepared for in each school.

AS: e se mo dupe. Se e le so fun wa nipa awon nkan ti o wa entailed nipa training ti OYES fun awon eeyan ko to di wipe won bere community work?

AS: thank you. Can you tell us what the pre-deployment training entailed?

BI: ninu training ti a se nigba ye: bawo la se le wa self-reliant? And ki a mo nkan ti a ba n se…hardworking in any aspect of life they found themselves…

BI: it included training on self-reliance and competence…and to be hardworking wherever we were deployed

AS: ninu programme OYES yen, o ni awon sections ti o se pe leyin community work ti won deploy si, aspect wo ni won deploy yin si?

AS: The programme comprises various sections where people are placed after the community service phase, which was yours?

BI: emi ni mo head Osogbo Local government after some months. Mo ni oga nigba yen ti o koko head wa ni Local government sugbon issue kekere kan sele. Later won sa choose me pe kin take over. Being a prefect gbogbo aspects la maan participate ninu. Gbogbo deployment. We have …czar,we have environmental, we have sheriff guard, we have paramedic team, teaching. Leyin teaching ni a o participate. Every other aspect la n participate ninu. Teaching nikan ni mi o ni opportunity lati le participate but every other apect lan participate ninu. Even sheriff guard, ti Governor ba fe lo si ibikan, I will be there lati mo nkan to n sele nibe.

BI: I headed Osogbo Local Government after some months. I had a superior then but I was made to replace him due to some issues. Being a prefect, one functions in all the available sections. We have the environmental czar, sheriff guard, the paramedic team and teaching. It was in teaching alone I did not participate. I even had to be with the sheriff guards to supervise them anytime the governor goes on an outing.

AS: so prefect o need lati wa ni any specific aspect…a gbo pe ijoba ipinle osun won ko awon OYES kan lo si Cuba, e de ni anfani ati oreofe lati lo pelu won. S e le so die fun wa nipa e?

AS: therefore, the prefect does not have to belong in any of the sections. We learnt that the state government took some cadet members to

Cuba, and you happened to be one of them. Can you tell us a little about that?

AS: …ope ni fun Olorun. Ade dupe lowo Mr. governor, Ogbeni Rauf Aregbesola. Ti a ba ni kan flash back, issue OYES is like wipe o recognize youths ko de fe ki awon eeyan wa jobless. 10 thousand la n gba, yes but that particular 10 thousand to ba ti to time to ye ki a gba, 'se e ti ri alert?' awon eyan ma ma pe'ra wan ni…eyan ni sense of belonging pe atleast, ni end of the month nkan ma jade wa. Lori oro Cuba, surprise lo je fun mi because…less than a week ni mo sese mo pe Cuba la fe lo. Won kan pe mi, 'se o ni nkan bayi, boya national ID card?' mo ni mii ni. 'ki lo ni?' mo ni international passport. 'okay, fine, lo mu wa.' Mo de submit e sibe lai mo nkan ti won fe fi se. the first month, second month, third month. Moni, 'ah, e kan gba passport mi, e o so anything fun mi. e ba mi mu passport mi.' wo ni k'emi ma lo jare. Igba to de ya to ku less than a month ti a maa travel, won de pe wa pe… ki a se awon documentation kan. A sa se awon documentation. After that…boya bi three days or four days mo de receive call pe we are to report at Ola Oni centre for moving to Cuba. I was surprised. Won honor mi. a de take off…a lo. A de Cuba…Cuba is good, mi o ti experience npe an travel ri. Bo tie sepe a ti n try pe a fe travel tele ti Olorun o tii kadara, but igba ti state government de recognize wa ti Olorun de sope tiwon la maa ba lo. We were five in number ti a lo lati ipinle OYES from different Local Governments. I am from Osogbo, we have Rafiu from Ila, wer have Seun from Ede, one particular guy from Iwo and a particular guy from Ife. Cuba experience, life won so simple… although won ni challenges to sepe challenges won…style of living won yato si tiwa nibibayi. They have a problem with the US. US o je ki country Kankan o partner pelu won therefore gbogbo nkan ti won lo is what they have been using for long. Won ni maintenance culture. They are into farming. Farming won at least a particular person to ba ni farm land o le ni less than minimum of 2 acres of land. And each farm land has its own tractor. Ko de si bo se le wu ki tractor na old to, o si ma ma sise. Which means won ni maintenance culture. Ko dabi tiwa nibi bayi to se pe we Nigerians a o ni maintenance culture. It is one of the experiences ti a ni. then ninu research wa, a tun se research debi wipe the union leaders, bi won se je union yen won tun ni farm land: hectares of farm lands ni each province ti won de gba workers sibe. At the end of the day ti won ba harvest ti won ba ta ni international market gain ti won ba ri nibe, won a divide e into three: won de ma ko percentage kan fun government, awon na ma share percentage kan and the other third one won ma share fun awon workers. Ko le sele ni Nigeria. Boya ile to maa mo lola o, Olorun le se ko ribe. And they don't believe in government must do everything for us. Government support won. You cannot go to Cuba pe mo kan fe lo stay tori challenges ti won ni…won believe in their own production. They believe in handy work. Won believe npe nkan ti a ba se la ma je ninu e. aso ti a se la n wo. Won o ko aso wa lati foreign country Kankan.

BI: glory is to God. And much gratitude is due the Governor, Ogbeni Rauf Aregbesola. It would be noticed that the OYES programme is aimed at recognizing the youths and end unemployment. Yes, the monthly stipend is 10,000.00 Naira but when it is month end, we put calls across one to another in anticipation of whether anyone has received payment alerts. It gives us a sense of belonging and the joy that at the end of the month something is coming into the purse from somewhere. Now to the Cuba issue: it was a total surprise for me because, I did not have any idea I would be going there until about a week to departure. I was called and asked if I had a national ID card. I said no. I was asked further if I had an International Passport and I answered yes. I was asked to submit it without being informed why. I complied, but after a few months and there was no new as to why I was asked to drop the document, I got curious and went to ask what was happening and retrieve my passport but I was sent back. However, when it was about a month to the trip, we were invited to process some documents. About three days later, I received a call to report to Ola Oni Centre, from where we were to depart for Cuba. I was surprised and felt greatly honored. Cuba is good. I had never travelled outside the country before then; though I have made efforts in the past but it seemed God had destined that it was through OYES. We were five cadet members from different Local Governments. We were 5 in all. I am from Osogbo Local Government; we have Rafiu from Ila, Seun from Ede, a guy from Iwo and another from Ife. The Cubans live a very simple life style. They have challenges which make their way of life different from ours. They have problem with the US and the US has forbidden other countries from assisting them. Therefore, they rely on old but functional technologies. They have maintenance culture. They survive on farming and each farmer has at least two acres of land. Each farm land has a tractor which is always in a working condition no matter how old it is. That is an indication of a strong maintenance culture which is lacking here in Nigeria. It is one fascinating experience. In our research, we also discovered that the Union leaders practice agriculture regardless of their being unionists. They have farm lands: hectres of farm lands in each province, worked on by paid employees. At the end of each harvest, the produce is sold at the international market and the proceed is share into three with a percentage going to the government, another to the coffers of the union leaders to be shared as appropriate and the third goes to the payment of the worker's. That is a futuristic feat for a country like Nigeria. The Cubans also don't believe in waiting on the government to get things done for them; however the government is trying its best. One can not go to Cuba with a view to settling down there because of their problems but they believe in what they produce. They pay much premium to handy works. They believe in surviving on their own terms. They wear only those fabrics made in the country and do not rely on importation.

AS: …tin ba gbo yin dada, bi excursion ni irin ajo si Cuba je fun yin lati find out nipa lifestyle won, agriculture won ati manufacturing won, ki wa ni eyin, gege bi enikan to lo, ti o foju ri, ki ni ipa ti e le so pe o ti ni ninu life yin ati bi e se n se nkan gan?

AS: so the trip is for excursion purpose to expose you to their lifestyle, agriculture and manufacturing? As one who went and had such an experience, what observable impact has it had on you and the way you do things generally?

BI: e se mo dupe. Bi e se wole leekan, mo wa nidi production ni. kin to wo OYES mi o ni encouragement yen up to that but gradually an progress. Igba ti mo realize nkan ti mo lo se ni Cuba gaan, mo wa ri pe awon people yi won o ni anything. Government won se eyi to le se. mo de tun wa se awon research kan mo wa decide pe I will be a manufacturer.

BI: thank you. When you came in I left the production I was doing. Before I joined the OYES I did not have much encouragement but gradually I progressed. When I realized my mission to Cuba, I realized that they sustain themselves in spite of their scarcity. Their government tries its best. I also conducted some research and decided to be a manufacturer.

AS: so, what do you manufacture?

BI: presently I make soap, laundry soap. Bar laundry soap and I am thinking of starting my own factory. Apart from that mo nse body cream, hair cream. I can do anything cream.

BI: presently, I make soap: laundry soap; bar laundry soap. And I am thinking of starting my own factory. I also make body cream and hair cream. I have expertise in cream production.

AS: se e ti ko eleyi tele ki e to join OYES?

AS: have you learnt to do this before you joined the OYES?

BI: yes. OYES ko ni mo ti ko but OYES yen je kin… and experience travelling out tun je kin realize pe I can just do something on my own although I still work with the OAMBULANCE and the State Government. I am one of the prefects in OAMBULANCE…apart from that mi o je ki o discourage mi

BI: yes. I didn't learn this in the scheme but OYES exposed me to… and travelling to Cuba made me realize that I can start up something on my own; although, I still work with the O' AMBULANCE and the state government respectively. I am one of the prefects in O' AMBULANCE.

AS: …ki a to maa lo, ma fe ki e gba ijoba ni imoran rampe lori eto OYES

AS: lastly, I want you to advise Government briefly on the OYES programme

BI: mo dupe lowo Governor, Ogbeni Aregbesola and Commandante. Every time ni won maan high moral wa pe, 'anything you know, just do it. Come out and prove yourself.' Thank God, mentality yen si wa ni ara mi. mo maa ro State Government lati ri pe any Government to ba de ko ma scrape OYES because OYES o support many youths out there. They have a lot of programmes ti won se nibe…to de n ko awon eeyan lorisirisi ise; handy craft works. Mo ma enjoin government lati je ki…ki Olorun ran awon government lowo because nowadays, things are not…ki won try lati put more efforts. Awon eeyan benefit generally. Ko si family house kan, indigene or no indigene, won benefit nibe. Ari Yoruba, ari Ijaw, a ri hausa, a ri igbo ti won benefit nibe. Even igba ti second batch de, tori emi ni mo se registration fun won, mo le ka oye Hausa to wa nibe. Hausa community ati igbo community ti won benefit lara OYES ni Osogbo Local Government ati other Local Governments na.

BI: I thank the Governor, Ogbeni Rauf Aregbesola and the Commandante. They always encourage us to make the best use of our talents and abilities. They have always challenged us to prove ourselves. That attitude remains with me still. I will advise the State Government to ensure that the programme is sustained even after the end of this administration because, the OYES sustains many youths. They have a lot of programmes which enables the youths gain some skills and learn some trades and crafts. I will enjoin them that, with the help of God- because things are economically unfavorable- to put more efforts. The programme is beneficial to the populace. There is not a single household, indigene or non-indigene that does not benefit from it. Yoruba, Ijaw, Hausa and even Igbo communities are not left out in the numerous benefits.

APPENDIX VIII

INTERVIEW WITH MRS. LIASU SIMBIAT AJIBIKE

WUMI RAJI

LS: oruko temi ni Liasu Simbiat Ajibike

LS: my name is Liasu Simbiat Ajibike

WR: ewo ni surname nibe?

WR: which is your surname?

LS: Liasu ni surname, Simbiat- oruko musulumi l'obinrin. Ajibike ni oruko abiso. Mo wa lati ijoba ibile Boluwaduro ni ilu Iresi. Omobibi ilu Iresi ni mi ni ijoba ibile Boluwaduro. Mo wa se OYES ni Ifelodun local Government ni Ikirun

LS: Liasu is the surname. Simbiat is a Muslim name while Ajibike is my other name. I hail from Iresi in Boluwaduro Local Government. I am an indigene of Iresi. I took part in the OYES at Ikirun in Ifelodun Local Government.

WR: Odun wo niyen?

WR: what year was that?

LS: 2011

WR: first batch 2011 to 2013

LS: yes

WR: iwe melo lo ka?

WR: what is your educational qualification?

LS: college of education ni mo ti pari ni ila

LS: I graduated from College of Education, Ila

WR: course wo lo se?

WR: what did you study?

LS: Economics-Social Studies

WR: odun wo lo pari

WR: what year did you graduate?

LS: 2009

WR: ki lo de to fi je pe OYES ni o wa n se

WR: why then did you decide to opt for OYES in spite of your educational background?

LS: igba ti mo pari ni igba yen ko tii si repete, mo n sise ni private school. Igba ti wahala private school tie po to je wipe mo sise ni ibikan to se pe teacher o ni table ko ni chair. Won kan ma dide duro ko omo ni. Teacher fee le subu lori iduro. Igba ti wahala private school yen po mo tun lo sise ni hotel kan to wa ni Okini, Konkonbilo. Ibe ni mo wa

LS: when I graduated there was not much to do. I worked with a private school but the work condition was inhospitable. I worked in a particular school where teachers were not given the basic furniture to sit or write on. They had to stand around through out the day and some even almost collapse from exhaustion. When the stress was unbearable I got another job at Konkobilo Hotel in Okini.

WR: ki lo n je Konkonbilo?

WR: what does Konkobilo mean?

LS: Konkonbilo ni man yen name hotel house e…ibe ni mo wa ti mo ti gbo pe form yi o jade- form OYES. A de lo. Mo ni ka try e. Bo de je pe hotel na ni eeyan ma wa pelu qualification…dandan na sa leeyan fin struggle. Mo ba lo gba form, a submit. Igba to ya won so pe oruko wa ti jade o. a de lo. Mo wa lo si Ikirun fun training ni year yen. A de bere ni Ifelodun. Ati Osogbo ni mo ti maan lo si Ikirun tori Osogbo ni emi base si. Mo maan lo si Ikirun every day fun duty mi ni ibe tori a ma gba'le, a ma tun oja se, tun gbogbo e se nigba yen. Ise ti a maan se niyen

LS: the man simply named his hotel Konkonbilo. I was working there when the OYES form was released. I gave it a try even though I remained at the hotel. One just has to keep struggling. I obtained the form and submitted it. Later I learnt that my name came out on the list. So, I went for training at Ikirun that year. I worked at Ifelodun. I went from Osogbo to Ikirun because I was based here in Osogbo. I resumed duty at Ikirun every day because I was allocated portions to sweep. We did sanitation works at the market.

WR: igba ti e pari training eyin naa koko…

WR: when you completed the training

LS: a sise. A gba'le…won maan fun wa ni ile sisan. But group ti won pin wa si awon okunrin wa maan assist nipa ile sisan; tori ile egbe titi won maan ni ki a saan…igba ti mo tie koko n se ise yen gbogbo owo mi lo fa ya tori oko egbe titi.

LS: we worked. We swept…we also cut portions of verges although the men in our group helped out with the cutting most times. In fact, when I first started my hands were sore ridden due to grass cutting.

WR: sugbon o ni o n sise ni hotel kan tele, ise yen wa nko?

WR: but you said you were working at a hotel, what happened to that?

LS: igba ti oruko ti jade…

LS: I got selected for OYES

WR: se iyen tun wa better hotel yen ni?

WR: was that any better compared to the hotel job?

LS: se e mo pe ise ti ijoba, eyan a wo pe from there Olohun le se ki iyen o permanent. Better offer na lo je ka kuro ni ibeyen. Even awon ti a jo sise ni hotel yen awon imiin o kuro: igba ti won ti ni ise ile gbigba ni won maa ma se, awon o le se. Emi wo pe at least ti a ba de ibe, Olohun le se ki ari better offer to permanent die

WR: I considered that being a government; it has a possibility of being permanent. I left the hotel looking for a better offer. Some people who also got selected refused to leave the hotel job when they discovered that the new job involves sweeping streets. I felt this could actually be precursor to better and permanent job offers.

WR: bawo lo se ri ni ara tie na nigba ti won koko so pe ile ni e maa ma gba?

WR: how did you feel when you learnt that the job involves sweeping streets?

LS: won so. won so pe ile la maa ma gba mo sope to,se won sa maa ma fun wa l'owo. Kii se pe a maama gbale ni ati aaro di ale; o sa maa ni iye Asiko ti a fi maa gba ti a de ma lo'le wa. Olohun de le se nigba ti a ni nkan lowo ti a n se, wo le fe gba eeyan ki won wo tiwa pe…tori pe ise ti ijoba yato si ti private something

LS: we were informed of the job specification and I said, 'well, as long as we will be paid for it and it is not going to last all day.' The work is time bound and afterwards we can go back to our homes. Who knows, other better and more permanent positions could open while we are doing this. Government job is actually different and better that any private job.

WR: o to igba wo ti e fi gbale?

WR: how long did the sanitation works last?

LS: emi gba ile o ku die ko pe 2 years

LS: I was on it for about 2 years

WR: o tumo si pe sanitation czar ni won gbe e si tele tele

WR: that implies that you were in the Sanitation Czar

LS: sanitation ni a koko maan fi bere

LS: we all started with sanitation works

WR: mo mo iyen, sugbon leyin igba yen won maan gbe yin kuro nibe

WR: I know that but after that, cadets are deployed to other places

LS: igba ti mo gba ile yen, o ku die ki 2 years pe ki won to gbe wa lo si Genenral Hospital ni Ikirun, a se training fun sheriff guard. Sheriff guard la se training fun ki won to ko wa lo si General Hospital

LS: I had swept for about 2 years before we were transferred to the General Hospital at Ikirun. We were trained as sheriff guards before we were sent to General Hospital.

WR: ibo le ti se training fun sheriff guard?

WR: where did you undergo the training?

LS: a koko se training ni Ilesa. Won really organize training yen. Awon soldiers train wa. Won fun wa ni handout. Won maan lecture wa ni ibeyen. A se training ni NYSC camp l'ede.

LS: we were first trained at Ilesa. It was a well coordinated programme. It was coordinated by soldiers who lectured and gave us instructional materials. We had drills at the NYSC camp, Ede as well.

WR: general training ni iyen?

WR: that was a general training then?

LS: general training ni. All local governments lo se iyen to je sheriff corps ti won select ninu OYES ni won se

LS: yes, it was. All OYES cadet members selected for the sheriff corps took part in the training.

WR: bawo ni won se select eni to je sheriff corps?

WR: how were you all in the sheriff corps selected?

LS: kii se pe o much na. won kan maa ni ki a wa si parade fun awon training kan to tun yato fun ti ile gbigba pe eni to ba fe wa ni sheriff o, ki o wa. A de maa lo. Boya two days in a week o ni a fi maan se. igba to ya la to n se ni local governments wa. Won a pe gbogbo local government ojo ti a ba maa lo si ilesa, ojo ti a ba ma lo si ede. The last one ti a se, o dabi eniipe awa ti first batch yen kini lati se, Governemnt House. soldiers, mopol gbogbo won naa wa pelu Ogbeni won se final something nigba yen.

LS: it was nothing much. We were asked to come for parade for the basic training that is totally different those given for the sanitation works. We attended for about two weeks. We later continued the training at our various Local Governments. All Local Governments were notified when to converge at Ilesa or Ede training centres. The last session we had was, I suppose for the first batch, at the Government House. Soldiers ,Mopol and all were present with Ogbeni for the final parade.

WR: ki ni training yin entail?

WR: what did you training entail?

LS: won so wipe won maa create state security naa nigba yen. Oun lo je ki awon eeyan rush in wipe at least awa ti Governor select as sheriff yi boya a le benefit lati ara state security

LS: they said they were going to create a state security then. that was responsible for the rush to apply. We thought that at least, we who were selected by the Governor for the sheriff corps expected to have preferential consideration when recruitment for the state security commenced.

WR: igba ti e pari training tan nko?

WR: and when you completed the training?

LS: igba ti a pari training, won wa pin wa si GMT.

LS: when we completed the training we were deployed to the GMT

WR: nigba wo ni e ti wa ni bi?

WR: and since when have you been here?

LS: emi ti koko wa nibi lati 2012. Late 2012 lati koko de ibi. Government house la koko maan lo. A ba Ogbeni lo si outing like two times. Igba to ya won ni Annex ni won maa ko wa lo. Oya won wa ni ibi bayi, awa fo ibi, a wa wa si ibi. Igba ti awa wa nibi yi, awa first batch yen won da awa first batch yen si'le- awa 50 niwa. awon to train leyin wa, ibi ni won ti se training fun awon ati Islaudeen nibi ati inu ogba ni ibi ni won ti se training fun won. Won wa mu lara won. Awa lo. Some months later won tun pe wa pada pe eni to ba ni interest, a tun wa pada wa. Awa first batch yen boya ni a ju five lo nibi bayi…emi nikan ni obinrin to je firsrt batch.

LS: I have been here since 2012. We have been brought here since late 2012. At first we were at the Government House. We accompanied Ogbeni to some outings on about two occasions. Later, we heard they were going to send us to Government Annex but eventually we were brought here. When the time was up we the first batch passed out: about 50 of us. Those who came on the second batch were trained here and on the premises of Islahudeen School. The successful ones amongst them were selected. Some months later, we were called back. Interested ex-members were encouraged to apply. Those of us who served in the first batch are barely more than 5 on the team presently. I am the only female left.

WR: ki wa ni ise yin gege bi GMT; ki le wa da le lori?

WR: what is your job specification at GMT?

LS: ise wa naa ni wipe, awon olopa to je Govenor Monitoring team ati civil defense o je three organisation: police,civil defense and sheriff guards. Awa sheriff guards la je third organisation si police and civil defense. So, movement governor ni won monitor ni GMT. Anywhere governor is, we suppose to be there. Ti won ba tiin lo a ma tele won. Igba kan nibi bayi, a sise nipa awon to n se mining, illegal mining. Nigba ti a se first batch, awon ti won se kini yen won ma lo wa gold yen illegally to je pe governor o mo nipa e. a maan lo mu won. A ma fa won fun ijoba.

LS: our job is to serve as the third art of the Governor Monitoring Team which comprises the Police, Civil Defense Corps and us. We monitor the Governor's movements. Anywhere the Governor is, we are expected to be there. We go with him wherever he goes. Sometime ago, we cracked down on people involved in illegal gold mining activities without the Governor's consent. We arrested and handed them over to the police.

WR: nibo ni won tin wa gold yen?

WR: where exactly was this gold mining taking place?

LS: a ri ni side Ilesa; Ijesa side ni a ti se iyen ju. A ma round won up, a ma ko won lo fun ijoba. Nigba yen o ti pe but a o se iyen mo. Nigba yen bi 2013-14 ni a ti se iyen last. a tun se awon alalamole

LS: it was around Ilesa. We rounded them up and handed them over to the police. That was some years ago. We no longer do that. The last time we embarked on such a mission was 2013-2014. We also worked on illegal loggers.

WR: ki lon je be?

WR: what does that mean?

LS: won ma kan lo ge igi ti won o ko lo si ibi ti won ti nse ni awon plank kini…ti won ti n fi nkan lu; awon ti o stamp. Inu igbo ni won ti ma age ni won ti maa la. Won maa gbe lo ta

LS: they usually went and cut down tress without proper authorization from the right places; without stamp duties. They cut and log right in the forest and went from their straight to sell.

WR: illegal logging?

LS: illegal logging. A se iyen naa nigba yen. A maa mu won; a maa mu won lo si nearest police station ibi ti a ba ti mu won naa ni. so, ijoba maa gbo si. A o se iyen mo ni isin yi

LS: illegal logging. We also fought that. We arrested them and took them to the nearest police station. That way Government The officers explain that the informant was shot with an unregistered bullet shortly before they arrived the scene. Know about such things. But all that has ceased too.

WR: ki wa ni koko ise ti en se bayi?

WR: what exactly do you do now?

LS: bayi, nkan ti a nse nibi na ni wipe…iru ni isin yi bayi, ni ale oni 31st, Ogbeni fe se fire work ni freedom park, GMT must be there. That is why ti a fi wa ni ibiise ni ale yi pe a fe lo si'be. Movement Ogbeni- ibi to ba lo na ni a n lo. Mi o wa mo boya awon oga wa to je olopa o, there might be another work or assignment ti won tun n se

LS: right now, like today is 31st, the Governor has firework display to do at the Freedom Park tonight, GMT must be there. That is why we have reported for duty this evening. Ogbeni's movement is our business; wherever he goes, we go. I don't know if our superiors in the police have any other engagements tonight

WR: awon olopa naa tun maan fun yin ni ise miin?

WR: do the police officers assign responsibilities to you as well?

LS: rara. ise governor naa ni

LS: no. it is what ever the Governor wants

WR: eelo ni won wa n fun yin?

WR: how much is your take home pay?

LS: governor n san salary hadoc bi salary yen se bere lati ibere 10 thousand ni won n san fun wa; lati inu Governemnt House. igba ti awon first batch wa nibi yi gan 15 thousand ni won n fun wa by hand. Igba yen first batch, 2 years wa ti pe fun OYES. Won de n san 15 thousand fun wa by hand. Nigba yen, as at 2014 ni iyen ti lo. Igba ti o ma ya, ti awon first batch ti lo ti second batch ti de, won fun won ni 10 thousand OYES yen directly tori owo won o tii stop nigba yen. Won wa n fun wa ni 2000- 2000 from Government House every month

LS: Governor pays us ad hoc salary as it has been since inception. We are paid 10 thousand naira from the Government House. The pay was 15 thousand naira paid in cash when the first batch were still here. We still got the 15 thousand monthly stipends for services rendered even after our 2 years OYES service. That regime ended in 2014. When the second batch came on, the OYES still got their 10 thousand naira as usually directly from the Government House so it extends to those in the GMT. We however got additional 2 thousand naira in cash from Government House every month.

WR: so, kii se pe won n san si account yin?

WR: so, it is not paid into you bank accounts?

LS: account ni owo OYES n wole si every month; that 10,000. But 2000 by hand ni. o maa wole papo pomo allowance police ati civil office wa nibi.

LS: the OYES 10 thousand naira stipends still come through our bank accounts every month. Additional 2 thousand naira is paid by cash along with the salaries of the police and civil defense officers on the team.

WR: o ni won fun yin ni 15000 by hand nigba yen

WR: you said you were paid 15 thousand naira cash then

LS: by hand ni. ni igba ti 2 years ti OYES ti stop nigbayen, 2011-2013 by han ni won fun wa. 10 ni won koko n fun wa by hand but later won tun so di 15000. Like some months boya 6- 5 months ni a fi gba 15 yen by hand ki won to wa stop ki a to lo. Won da wa'le. Igba ti awon wa de leyin wa; second batch wa de, 10000 lo n wole fun won ni OYES tori'pe OYES ti won oi ti stop. Won sin gba salary. Won wa n fun won ni 2000 lati Government House. 2000 yen lawa na n gba.

LS: yes, during the 2011-2013, we received payment by hand but that stopped after the lapse of the 2 year term. At first it was 10 thousand before it was eventually increased to 15 thousand. I think we got the

15 thousand pay for about 5-6 months before it stopped. We passed out. When the second batch resumed they got 10 thousand naira from OYES because their cadet accounts were still operational. The GMT amongst them got the regular 10 thousand naira and got additional two thousand in cash. That extends to us.

WR: ki ni impression e nipa OYES; o ti wa ni OYES lati bi odun merin bayi?

WR: you have been on the programme for about 4 years now, what is your opinion about OYES?

LS: emi o tie le fi enu buruku soro OYES, tori bo se wu ko ri, tori, koda ko se university graduate ni mi nigba yen, sebi eni to ba ri ise lo ma ranti pe oun tie lo school ri debi wipe oun Kankan per month. Bi awon eeyan se so to pe ile ni, pe awon ọ le je ki omo awon gbale; ibi ti ori ba da enikookan si la ma gbe. Igba to ni ka gba o saa n fun wa ni nkankan. Ko de je ki ebi ko pawa... mo ti ri ojo ti alert wole bayi to je pe oti di late hour,bo se di aaro ojo keji bayi mo lo gba ni, mo de na tan. Reason ni pe ko si nkankan ni ile. Omo mi jeun. Tori mo ti l'omo ko to di pe mo gba OYES

LS: I can never pass a negative comment on OYES because it has provided me an opportunity to be employed. One's education is irrelevant unless one is gainfully employed. However people disregarded it as mere street sweeping and they wouldn't allow their kids do it, one has to accept one's lot and do what has to be done. Beside, it is a means of earning a pay and a decent living. There was a time that the bank alert came late in the night. Early the following morning, I went out to withdraw it and spent it up immediately because we were badly in need of supplies at home. My children were fed. I have had kids before I joined OYES

WR: o ti marry?

WR: you are married?

LS: mo ti marry.

LS: yes

WR: omo melo lo ni

WR: how many kids do you have?

LS: omo meta

LS: three

WR: how old are they

LS: oun ti wa ni boya bi SS 1 nigba yen but now o ti pari. Aburo e keji na fe se WAEC bayi. Oun naa ti san owo fun kini. Won ni to ba pass awon ma return owo e fun wa. Kekere wa ni JS 3. Kekere yen private school lo wa nigbayen ni primary class nigba ti mo gba OYES. Oun na ni mo de fi n manage ara mi. tori obirin lemi bi jo. Iyen lo je ki oko da mi nu pe, obirin lemi bi o. mo de n da nkan mi gbe

LS: she was in SS 1 then but now she has finished from the secondary school. The younger one is about to write WAEC now. We have paid for the exam and expect a refund from Government if she passes. The youngest of them is in JS 3 presently. She was in a private primary school when I joined the OYES. It is through this job that I have been coping with all these responsibilities. All my three children are females so my husband abandoned me for that. I have been grappling with it all by myself

WR: so oko re ti ni iyawo miin bayi?

WR: so, your husband has taken another wife

LS: tipe

LS: yes, since a long time ago

WR: se iwo ni number one abi?

WR: are you his first wife?

LS: emi ni o. emi la jo ferawa ni kekere

LS: I am his first wife. We started out since we were young

WR: melo lo wa fe le e bayi?

WP: how many more wives has he taken after you now?

LS: mi o tie mo iye won, tori o ti to 10 years ti a ti daru

LS: I don't know for sure because it has been over 10 years since we went our separate ways

WR: e pele. Ti won ba ni ki o gba ijoba ni imoran lori oro OYES, ki ni imoran ti o maa gba won?

WR: really sorry about that. If you had the chance to advise Government on OYES, what would you recommend?

LS: imoran ti maa kan gba won naa ni pe, ise ti OYES n se ni ilu ise to ni meaning ni. bi ijoba se introduce OYES o wa okay dada. Normal thing ni. ti won ba tun fe maa te siwaju bi won se so pe won fe gba OYES, ki won tun gba ni iwonba. Won tun ilu se. environment n neat. Advice mi fun won naa ni pe won si le te siwaju lati gba OYES. Ti won ba fe se recruitment miin, won le se. ojo keji ti won se Christmas ni Igbona nibeyen, ti e ba ri bi ibeyen se ri. Igba ti mo fi ma pada de ibe ni irole, o ti clear.

LS: the important contribution of OYES in society can not be overstated. The scheme is quite relevant and a step in the right direction. Going forward, I suggest they should still keep the number of intakes small. They perform essential social services and keep our environment clean. My advice is that they should go ahead with the programme. For instance, the day after Christmas, Igbona was a total eye sore due to wastes generated during the festivities but by the time I got back there in the evening, all the wastes had been cleared.

WR: OYES lo de sise yen?

WR: and the work was done by OYES?

LS: awon na ni; tori OYES lo lo si OWMA ti won ngbe motor kaakiri ti won fiin clear ile. From OYES ni won gba de ibeyen. So introduce ti won introduce OYES wa okay.

LS: yes they did it. It was OYES that went to collect trucks at OWMA to clear the refuse. They went through OYES. So, the scheme is a worthwhile initiative.

WR: sorry, ibeere kan wa ti mo fe beere leekan ti mo ti gbagbe. Oni awon nkan ti o ti gbe se ni idi OYES

WR: sorry, there is a question I need to have asked you but skipped my mind. You stated that you have achieved some things through OYES

LS: se e ri, ti eeyan ba wa laye, to ba ko ile to ra motor, mi o ju bi mo se wa yi naa lo- pempele- ti o ba l'omo ti o to omo re, wasted ni. ni isin yi, mo ji laaro, omo mi ri nkan je, o gba school lo; omo ti mo n fun lounje yen ni ile temi ati motor mi. ti omo mi o ba ti ku…inu ise yi, mi o sise imiin, ni mo fi ran omo mi lo se IJMB ni Ilorin- a year nibe. 200 level lo ma wole si ni university; ni UniIlorin. Nigba ti iru eyi ti mo n se yen ba ti wa mi o le gbadura ki o baje ti Olorun o ba ti pa, ise ti mo fi owo yen se o baje niyen. Emi naa de n live. So ara awon nkan ti mo fi se naa niyen… tori Yoruba ni ile ti a fi ito mo, iri laa wo. Ti mo ba ni ehn, iru OYES, bi won se fun mi lowo to o, omo mi o jeun o, ki won maa rin ka. Iru bi won se je obinrin yen awon naa a ti bi to eyo kookan. A o wa jo maa tele rawa ka. Ko ni meaning. Rubbish ni. sugbon nigba ti a le so pe e gba o, e se bayi, ti oun naa de n lo school. O ni project. Nkanto je koko ti emi fi se niyen…

LS: no matter one's lofty achievements, if one does not have a child or the ability to train that child, it is a waste. I wake up in the morning and can feed my children, and can send them to school; those children are my valuable achievements if they survive. It is through this job that I was able to send my daughter to do a year IJMB in the University of Ilorin. He is going straight to 200 level at the University of Ilorin. If all that has been possible, I have no reason to wish that the scheme come to naught. That is the source of my livelihood. If I had failed to invest in my children in spite of my OYES pay, they are females, they could have become teenage mothers themselves. That should truncate our growth potentials. But since I could cater for them, and send them to school, I am quite fulfilled and that is an important achievement for me.

WR: e se mo dupe. Kini oruko e leekan si?

WR: thank you so much. What is the name again?

LS: Liasu Simbiat Ajibike

APPENDIX IX

AN INTERVIEW CONDUCTED WITH MR. SULAIMAN SHERIFDEEN OLAIDE

WUMI RAJI

WR: Wumi Raji loruko mi. mo n se research kan lori OYES ni. Research ti mo de n se gbogbo awon to wa ni idi OYES ni won mo si, including commandante, including the Governor. Mo de ti interview awon OYES cadet bi tiyin naa. Mo koko fe ki o so oruko e fun mi

WR: my name is Wumi Raji. I am conducting a research on OYES, which is well approved by Commandante and as well as the Governor himself. I want you to first tell me your name

SO: oruko mi ni Sherifdeen Olaide

SO: my name is Sherifdeen Olaide

WR: igbawo lo koko bere pelu OYES

WR: when did you first enroll on the OYES?

SO: mo bere OYES lati 2011

SO: I started OYES in 2011

WR: 2011? that is first batch. Okay, bawo ni o se gbo nipa OYES, bawo I o se wo ibe?

WR: 2011? That is first batch. Okay, how did you get to know about OYES? How did you get enlisted?

SO: OYES je ise ti o wa okay; to le ise jina

SO: OYES is a very good job that end poverty

WR: bawo ni o se mo nipa e. igba ti won koko bere, o dabi pe won so pe ki e gba form. Igba ti e de gba form nko?

WR: how did you become aware of OYES; when the scheme started, you were directed to obtain some form. What happened after that?

SO: igba ti a gba form won supplement wa, won mu mi. igba ti won mu mi tan, a se training. Igba ti a se training tan a se data capture. After igba yen la to bere ise

SO: after we obtained the form, we were shortlisted. Then I was taken. After then, we were trained and data capture. It was after all that the we commenced work

WR: igba ti e bere ibo ni won gbe e lo?

WR: where were you posted to when you started work?

SO: mo bere sini sanko. Oni kini kan ti won pe ni daily portion

SO: I cut grasses. It was something termed daily portion

WR: sanitation Czars

SO: sanitation Csar. Ibe ni a ti koko bere. A bere si ni san oko egbe titi.

SO: yes. That was where we started. We cut grasses on the road verges

WR: iyen ni won maan fun gbogbo…

WR: that was general duty

SO: iyen ni general work ti everybody maan se ni OYES

SO: that is the general assignment given to every new member in OYES

WR: osu melo ni o fi se iyen

WR: how many months did you spend doing that?

SO: mo se iyen larin odun kan.

SO: I spent about a year on that

WR: odun kan ni o fi se iyen? Leyin igba yen wa nko?

WR: and after that?

SO: leyin igba yen ni mo gba leta lati wa ni GMT. GMT ni mo wa ti mo ti n serve bayi

SO: it was after then that I got letter of deployment to GMT. I am currently serving at GMT

WR: odun wo ni o ti wa ni GMT?

WR: since when have you been on the GMT?

SO: mo ti wa ni GMT lati 2010

SO: I have been on GMT since 2010

WR: 2010 ke? 2011 ni…o ni o lo odun kan ni…boya 2012 lo koko de ibi

WR: 2010? 2011 seems more accurate since you said you spent a year cutting grasses. Perhaps, 2012 is your actual year of deployment

SO: 2014. Mo de GMT ni 2014

SO: 2014. I got to GMT in 2014

WR: as OYES cadet ti won gbe wa si GMT, ki ni koko ise ti e n se yato si oko ti e ti san teletele?

WR: as an OYES cadet member deployed to GMT, what exactly is your work specification that is different from your grass cutting you held earlier

SO: bi a se wa ni GMT bayi: Governor's Monitoring Team ni won pe wa. Anywhere ti Governor ba ti n lo within Osun State a maan tele governor lo lati ba won sise nibe. Crowd ni won gba wa fun lati maa ba won control crowd tori awon olopa to wa nibe, won o le gbe ibon dani lati maa control crowd. Lati maa le awon ero ki won ma disturb ti Governor ba n sise.

SO: we are called the Governor's Monitoring Team. Anywhere the Governor goes within Osun State, we always go with him. we are employed to control the crowds at events, the police can not control the crowds while holding their guns. So we help keep the crowd back so as not to disturb the Governor's programme.

WR: ti Governor o ba wa lo si ibikan nko?

WR: what happens when the Governor has no outing to go to?

SO: ti Governor o ba lo si ibikan, a maan wa ni office wa. A maan se morning duty nibe a de maan se night duty.

SO: if the Governor has no outing to go to, we stayed in our office. We do morning and night duties there

WR: kini morning duty yen je?

WR: what is the morning duty about?

SO: morning duty yen wa fun pe ki a ko ise awon olopa; ki a wa laarin won. Anywhere la le ba arawa lola. Eko laan fi iyen ko laarin wa. A de maan pe kini kan na ni standby. Eni ti o ba si ni morning duty ti o de si ni night o maa wa ni standby; to sepe ti Governor ba fe jade awon lo ma tele Governor jade.

SO: the morning duty entails us working closely with the police; to mingle with them to acquire skills that should be useful for us in the future. We also have something known as standby. Any member who is not on either the morning or night duty is kept on standby incase the Governor need to go somewhere urgently. The standby people go with him.

WR: so, ti e o ba si ni duty nkan ti e nse ni pe e n ko die nipa ise olopa. S e o feel pe nkan ti e n ko yen le se anfaani fun yin?

WR: so, when you are not on duty, you learn from the police? Do you feel that things you are learning there could be of any use to you?

SO: bee ni

SO: yes

WR: iru anfaani wo?

WR: of what benefit can that be?

SO: iru anfaani to le se fun wa naa ni wipe a le ni a o ni sise olopa ki a ba ara wa nibe lola. A le sope a o ni se soja ki a barawa nibe lola. Tori GMT ti a wa yi, a se training ki o to di pe a di GMT. Ti o ba wa di ola nisin yi ti a ba fe join olopa tabi soja ni, ti iru training yen ba pada je jade, ko ni nkan ti o niwa lara ki a to le perform iru training yen

SO: the benefits include preparing us for the possibility of a job in either the police or the military; who knows where we could find ourselves later? The training we are given in the GMT can become handy if we later decide to the police or the military, when similar skills are required. It should make qualifying easier for us.

WR: iru training wo ni e se ki won to ko yin wa GMT?

WR: what type of training did you receive before you were deployed to GMT?

SO: won train wa ni ori field

SO: we were trained on the field

WR: ori field wo?

WR: on what field?

SO: ori field islahudeen Grammar School.

SO: on the field of Islahudeen Grammar School.

WR: iru training wo ni won se fun yin?

WR: what type of training were you given?

SO: a perform march-past. Some many other training like that. Won o kowa bi won se n yinbon. Bi a sele defend ara wa; self defense. Ti ija ba de nibi ti a ti n control crowd, bi a sele escape, gbogbo e ni won ko wa nibe

SO: we learnt march-past and such other trainings. We were not taught how to use guns but we were tutored how to defend ourselves in case of a unrest in the course of our duty. We were taught how to escape unhurt.

WR: leyin pe e n control crowd nibi ti Governor ba lo, ki tun ni ise ti e nse gege bi GMT?

WR: besides crowd control wherever the Governor goes, what other work do you do as GMT?

SO: ko si ise miin ta n se ju pe ti a ba t igbo oro ti won so ni ita nipa Governor, ani awon iko kan ti won pe ni surveillance larin wa

SO: nothing other than gathering intelligence reports and feedbacks concerning the Governor. We have intelligence officers amongst us who do such surveillance duties.

WR: otele muye

WR: secret agents?

SO: be ni. ti a ba ti gbo ti won soro Governor laida tabi ijoba ipinile generally laida, a ni lati report case yen.

SO: yes. Anywhere we hear people talking badly about the Governor or the state Government at large, we report the case.

WR: eyin lo je bi eti oba nile, eti oba loko. Okay, eyin ni eyan to wa nibe. Yato fun wipe e n control crowd e tun collect information fun ijoba. Ki wa ni feeling e nipa GMT ti won gbe e si yi?

WR: so, you are like the Governor's informant. You perform the dual function of crowd control and intelligence gathering, what is your feeling about the GMT where you currently are?

SO: mo dupe lowo Olorun pe mo wa ni GMT tori pe opo eyan lo fe debe ti won o ri oreofe lati de be. Mo fe jeun, mo n ri ounje je lasiko. Mo fe mu, mo n ri mu lasiko.

SO: I thank God for being on the GMT because it is the envy of a lot of people. Making ends meet has been very easy for me.

WR: elo ni won n fun yin losu.

WR: how much is your monthly pay?

SO: allowance ti OYES ti won wa ni igboro ti won n san'le. The same salary ni a jo n gba. 10 thousand naira ni a jo ngba but awa n receive special allowance nibi bayi to je 2 thousand naira per month

SO: we are paid the same amount as normal OYES members who cut grasses. We get paid the uniform 10 thousand naira with 2 thousand naira special monthly allowance.

WR: awon wo lo n fun yin ni special allowance

WR: who gives you the special allowance?

SO: iyen n wa lati odo ijoba ipinle Osun.

SO: that comes from the state Government

WR: iyen mean n pe e ni awon advantage kan ju awon ti won gbe lo si ibo min? o ni o bere lati 2011, o wa ti to odun melo ti o ti bere sini se OYES?

WR: that means that you have some advantages over those in other areas of deployment. You said you started since 2011, for how long have you been in OYES?

SO: odun keje

SO: seventh year

WR: 2011? Odun marun ni iyen. Omo ibo ni yin?

WR: 2011? This should be the fifth year. Where are you from?

SO: omo ipinle Osun naa ni

SO: I am from Osun State

WR: ni'bo?

WR: Where in Osun?

SO: omo bibi Ifetedo ni mi

SO: I hail from Ifetedo

WR: Ifetedo, ibo ni Ifetedo wa?

WR: ifetedo, where is that located?

SO: Ifetedo wa ni Ife South Local Government, after Garage Olode, boundry Ondo State ati Ipinle Osun

SO: Ifetedo is in Ife in Ife South Local Government, after Garage Olode, at the boundary of Ondo and Osun States.

WR: okay. Ki ni qualification?

WR: okay. What is your qualification?

SO: SSCE ni mo ni lowo

SO: SSCE

WR: ki lo wa de ti oo ka'we si?

WR: why did you not further your education?

SO: ko si agbara ko si si oluranlowo. Gbogbo erongba mi ni pe emi naa o ka iwe si sugbon niwonba igba ti mo sise yi, enu awon change kekeke ti mo ti realize mo ti gbiyanju lati further sugbon Olohun o ti kadara pe mo ri admission.

SO: I had neither the financial capacity nor assistance to do so. I strongly wish to acquire a higher education and I have spent my meager savings trying to realize the dream to no success.

WR: ki ni o ti tun gbe se leyin pe o fi owo pamo

WR: what else have you been able to achieve besides saving towards education?

SO: mo ni awon okada ti mo n gun funrami ti awon eyan de n ba mi gun.

SO: I bought some motorcycles which I ride for commercial transport services. I also lease them out for such purposes

WR: o se

WR: thank you

APPENDIX X

INTERVIEW WITH MRS TOYIN ADELEKE (CONDUCTED ON DECEMBER 2ND, 2016)

SADE ADEWALE - LAWAL

Sade: Hello, good morning ma. My name is Mrs. Folasade Adewale-Lawal. I am here representing Dr. Wumi Raji of Obafemi Awolowo University, Ile-Ife. I am here to conduct an interview with you regarding OYES. Ma, could you please give me background information about yourself?

Mrs. Adeleke: You are welcome ma. I am Adeleke Toyin. One of the OYES traffic marshals under the able governor, Ogbeni Rauf Aregbesola

Sade: Where are you from?

Mrs. Adeleke: I am a native of Osogbo

Sade: From which local government?

Mrs. Adeleke: Osogbo local government

Sade: Yes ma. Could you please tell me your educational background and how you found yourself in OYES (Osun Youth Empowerment Scheme)

Mrs. Adeleke: Thank you very much ma. I am a native of Osogbo in Osogbo local government. Before I joined OYES, I was working with Nigeria Machine Tools before it was later privatized by former president Olusegun Obasanjo. Immediately after the privatization of Machine Tools, I worked with Captain Cook. While working in Captain Cook, a customer once came, who informed me about OYES. He asked me to go to my local government to obtain the OYES form. I asked him if they were demanding for anything for the form

Sade: Anything like what?

Mrs. Adeleke: Money for the form. The man said the form was being given out at no cost. When I got to my local government, I got the form and filled it. Luckily for me, when the list was out, my name was also there and we later went for training

Sade: Do you mean the 3 weeks training?

Mrs. Adeleke: Yes, 3 weeks training. We did that at St. Charles. After the training, we were sent to Abere, under Ministry of Works and Transport

Sade: Immediately after the training?

Mrs. Adeleke: Yes. After the training we swept the floor. My portion was along Ataoja secondary school

Sade: For how long did you do that?

Mrs. Adeleke: For almost seven months or even eight months

Sade: Eight months!

Mrs. Adeleke: After 8 months, they redeployed us to OYES traffic marshal

Sade: Ok

Mrs. Adeleke: When we got to OYES traffic marshal, we were many, we were up to 70 cadets that were deployed to Traffic marshal. Lot of them then was asking then if their salary will be increased for closing by 4 pm? I told them the salary will not be increased. We were collecting #10,000 at the initial stage. When we got to traffic marshal, some said they cannot cope with the situation; closing by 4pm with #10,000 salary. So they went away. With all these, I endured. I was closing by 4pm and was receiving #10,000 at the end of the month. Our salary was increased to #15,000 and we were later given a permanent appointment

Sade: Sorry I forgot to ask, you are you among the 1st batch?

Mrs. Adeleke: Yes I am

Sade: So you joined OYES in 2011

Mrs. Adeleke: I can't even remember

Sade: From sanitation, you moved to ministry of works before you were deployed to OTRAM. Were you trained for the OTRAM assignment?

Mrs. Adeleke: Thank you so much ma, the question you asked me baffles me. When I joined OYES, people referred to me as "old cargo" meaning an old woman. When we were deployed to traffic marshal, we were given 2 weeks training which I endured. People were amazed at my performance that they asked if I had worked as police traffic warden before then. I replied them that,"ebi ati iya lo ko mi l'ogbon" meaning I was trained by hunger and poverty. Hunger and poverty trained me to hard work.

Sade: It is not everyone that passes through hard times that would learn from their experience. It is just your person. I also noticed that you are so popular among other marshals with the way you control traffic. Have you ever received anything in recognition for your hardwork?

Mrs. Adeleke: About that, an award was given to me by Primus magazine. That was in November 2013. Another one was given to me by Rotary club in September 2016. The Rotary club gave me additional assistance. The chairman of Rotary club, Mr. Dapo Oyedele asked me questions that brought out tears from me, thinking about what life has taught me. He also asked me about how I got to work so hard and control the traffic distinctively. As usual, I told him I was trained by hunger and poverty

Sade: Ever since I noticed you at work, you are this cheerful and friendly person. You can easily be noticed with the manner in which you discharge your duty. Hunger and poverty cannot teach that!

Mrs. Adeleke: I have focus and determination

Sade: Good. So the award you were talking about, one from Primus magazine and the other one from the Rotary Club, how are they connected to OYES? Or they are not?

Mrs. Adeleke: I do not think they are connected, because the chairman of the Rotary club spotted me where I was controlling the traffic. I did not know him before then. He saw me and asked someone to call me for him, I went to him and he asked of my name. Jokingly, I said "OYES mama". He demanded for my real name and I told him Adeleke Toyin. He drove away without further question. It was on the award giving day that I got to know it was a meritorious award.

Sade: So the award was given based on recognition of your hard work?

Mrs. Adeleke: I think so

Sade: Yes it is. Because you said you met the man at your duty post. How about the Primus magazine award?

Mrs. Adeleke: The rotary club also gave my child a scholarship to the university level

Sade: In a way, we can still attribute the Rotary award to OYES. Because it was when OYES brought you to limelight, that the man saw your diligence which attracted a meritorious award

Mrs. Adeleke: Yes

Sade: Apart from the award achievement, which other personal achievement can you pinpoint?

Mrs. Adeleke: I thank God. Without Ogbeni Rauf Aregbesola, nobody will know me. Without OYES, I cannot be popular

Sade: Should we just say, OYES brought you to limelight?

Mrs. Adeleke: Yes

Sade: I don't know if you will like to tell me your educational qualification. You said you worked with Nigeria Machine Tools before joining OYES

Mrs. Adeleke: I am an HND holder. I studied elect at Osun State College of Technology, Esa Oke.

Sade: Is there any advice you have for the government on OYES or observation?

Mrs. Adeleke: I want to advice every one of us

Sade: OYES members?

Mrs. Adeleke: Not OYES members alone but everybody. Anywhere we find ourselves, we should be focused, determined and be ready to endure. We should be diligent in anything we do. We should not do things to impress people but rather discharge our duties as it is expected of us. Like myself, I am not working for my boss, but the entire people of Osun state

Sade: Thank you ma. Which area were you specialized in for the OYES exit programme? People specialized in photography, bead making, catering, e.t.c.

Mrs. Adeleke: There was no chance for me to do that because I will resume by 7am and close by 5pm. I will also take care of my children and husband. With all that, there won't be time for me to do any other thing

Sade: But you were aware of the exit programme?

Mrs. Adeleke: Yes

Sade: Thank you so much for granting me this interview. Do enjoy the rest of the day

Mrs. Adeleke: Thank you.

APPENDIX XI

INTERVIEW WITH MISS RUKAYAT ADEOLA FABUNMI (CONDUCTED ON 10TH JANUARY, 2017)

ADETOKUNBO ADEOLA SHITTU

AS: inu mi dun lati ba yin se if'orowanilenuwo yi.

AS: I am happy having this interview with you

RF: e se pupo. Inu temi na dun lati da yin lohun.

RF: thank you so much. I am equally elated to grant it

AS: ni akoko, maa fe ki e so fun wa nipa ara yin ni soki: oruko yin, qualification yin ati beebe lo

AS: first, I will like you to briefly tell us a little about yourself: your name, educational qualification, and so on

RF: oruko mi ni arabinrin Fabunmi Rukayat Adeola. Mo je omo bibi ilu Osogbo. Mo de ti ka iwe ni iwonba na; ati ka de ori NCE a de tun n se degree lowo ni University of Ilorin.

RF: my name is Miss Fabunmi Rukayat Adeola. I am a native of Osogbo. I hold an NCE and I am currently pursuing a first degree at the University of Ilorin

AS: e se mo dupe. A wa fe beere nipa OYES. A gbo pe e se OYES, mo fe ki e so die fun wa nipa e. bawo ni e se gbo nipa OYES?

AS: thank you. Now let us talk about OYES. We a aware that you participated in the OYES, I want you to tell us about this. How did you get to know about the scheme?

RF: mo gbo nipa OYES nigba ti ijoba gba mandate won pada ti won de se ileri pe awon ma gba OYES laarin ogorun ojo ti awon ba de ori ijoba. Igba yen mo si wa ni NCE, Ilesa, mi o lanfaani lati gba first batch. Igba ti a de ri akitiyan ti awon first batch se nigba yen lo je ki emi na gba second batch ti mo de si wa lenu e ti a n se programme ti won n pe ni adhoc lowo.

RF: I heard about it when the current Governor got his mandate back and promised to embark on the programme in his first 100 days in office. Then I was still on the NCE programme at Ilesa. I was not opportuned to enroll in the first batch. When we saw the impact of the first batch then, I was propelled to apply with the second batch and I have been involved in the scheme ever since. I am presently on the ad hoc.

AS: second batch yen lati odun wo si odun wo niyen?

AS: when did the second batch start and end?

RF: 2013 to 15

AS: iyen ni pe e pari batch yin ni 2015 e wa pada apply fun adhoc?

AS: in other words, your batch passed out in 2015 then you re-applied for the adhoc?

RF: bee ni

RF: yes

AS: ma fe ki e so fun wa nipa…agbo pe won se awon idanileko kan ki o to di wipe awon eeyan to bere sini sise; maa fe ki e so fun wa ni soki nipa idanileko na. ki ni awon ipele to wa ni ibe ati awon anfani wo ni e ri nibe ni soki?

AS: we heard that training was held before the cadets were deployed to work in the communities, I will like you to tell us briefly about the training. What were the segments and contents of the training, and what benefits did you derive there from?

RF: nipa idanileko, ni tooto ni won se idanileko sugbon ni titemi na, oruko mi pe die ko to jade; leyi ti won de ti bere training. So, mi o lanfaani lati ko ipa to poju nipa training. Later ni oruko mi sese jade ki won to pari but bi ojo bi meji abi meta to fi jade na, awa na bawon kopa nibi training. Idaji lati maa wa. Won ma se idanileko fun wa ni training; bi a sen n sare ni…lorisirisi. Igbayen ni won gba awon man o war fun wa ti won n ko wa. Leyin igba ti a ba se iyen tan la ma wo inu class ti won de ma lecture wa pelu iwe itoni ti won fun wa ni igba yen ki won to pin wa si enu ise.

RF: it is true that training was held but it had started before I was shortlisted. I missed a substantial part of the training phase but I was privileged to join them a few days to the end of the sessions. Activities for each day started at dawn: we jugged and did such other physical activities. Some Man O' War officers were engaged to handle that. After the exercises, we went into the class room where we were lectured based on the training Module given to us; before we got deployed at all.

AS: ki ni idanileko na da le lori ni soki?

AS: what do the lectures entail?

RF: o n je ki a mo koko elega mefa ti ijoba gun le to de wa ni ilana gege bi iwe ti won fun wa ti won fi n se idanileko fun wa; nipa bi a se le tan ise ohun osi, bi idagba soke se le wa nipa eto eko, bi ayika wa se le wa ni imototo ati beebe lo

RF: they familiarize us with the Government's 6 point agenda as outlined in the Module, which exposes how we could eradicate poverty, how to facilitate and attain growth in the educational sector, how to keep our environment clean, etc.

AS: eyin gege bi olukopa ninu eto OYES, e wa ni enu teaching bayi to niise pelu OYES, se e le so fun wa ni rampe bo se waye?

AS: as a participant in the OYES programme, who is currently on the O' TEACHER programme, can you enlighten us briefly how it happened?

RF: ni igba ti ijoba ti gbe eto OYES kale ni won pin ni isori isori. Ara e ni won ti yo awon traffic marshal, ibe ni won ti yo awon ti won pin si hospital ti won n ba ambulance sise. Ibe na ni won ti yo awa OTEACHERS ati awon eyan wa to wa ni environmental na. ni tooto na, nigba ti a bere ise, ki ijoba to pin wa, environmental ni gbogbo wa wa. Igba to ya ni wo n wo qualification ti onikaluku wa ni lowo. Oun ni won fi wa pin wa si ibi kookan. Iru awon to je pe healthtech ni won lo ni, awon yen ni won pe ni paramedics ti won ko won si hospital, ti won ko won si ambulance. Iru emi to sepe olukoni ni iwe eri owo mi ti a mo si NCE, won pin mi si ile iwe

RF: right from the onset, Government has designed OYES to have various sections. Amongst these are Traffic Marshal, and those deployed to the hospitals and those working with the ambulances. O-TEACHER is one of such sections and those in the environmental works. We were all first working in the environmental section before we were sent to other sections according to each cadet member's educational qualification. Those who have Health Tech were placed in the paramedics to work with the ambulances. I hold an NCE so I was deployed to teaching.

AS: se won kan wo sunsun won kan gbe yin lo si ile iwe ni abi o ni awon idanwo ti e se ko to di wipe e bere sii koni?

AS: were you just arbitrarily posted to teach or there was a form of exam to test your suitability before you were deployed?

RF: ni alakoko na, ni igba ti a n se screening ni local government eni kookan wa ni won ti mo ise ti onikaluku wa ni lowo. Nkan to koko sele pelu awon teacher ni wipe, mo lero pe nigba ti awon oga wa kookan feyin ti lenu eto eko ti awon aye wa ni awon ile iwe. Ijoba de ti se iwon to le se latari bi gbogbo nkan se ri, won ti gba awon eeyan. Ijoba tun wa wo pe awon omo OYES yi naa, awon ri awon to le se ise oluko ninu won. Oun ni won fi wa shortlist oruko awa kookan nigba yen ni won fi wa pin wa lo si schools. Sugbon nigba ti a pari second batch wa ti a n sise ti a mo si adhoc, won wa pada se exam fun wa ni October last year. Iyen ni won fi wa gba awa imiin to je wipe won ja awon ti won lero pe won o ye ni idi ise oluko. Awa ti won ro pe a si le maa ba awon sise, wo si fi awa sile.

RF: right from when we got screened at our various Local Governments, our qualifications have been noted. You know people continue to retire from both the civil service and teaching profession almost on a daily basis, and with this, there now are created vacancies that need to be filled. The state Government, having tried its best to employ the few new teachers that its declining resources allowed, considered the option of supplementing the shortage with qualified cadet members. That was how some of us got selected to teach in the schools. However, when the second batch ended and the idea of working on ad hoc basis started, an examination first had to be conducted. This was in October last year. That was how the least qualified to teach were sifted out and those of us considered qualified were retained.

AS: bawo ni won se n se koriya fun yin lenu eto OTEACHING?

AS: how is the remuneration for OTEACHERs?

RF: nipa OTEACHING; ni bayi ni tooto, Olohun la n be ko siju anu wo awa ti won pin si ile iwe. Gege bo se je pelu awon eeyan wa to wa ni sanitation ise wa ni pe larin ago meje si ago mewa; wakati meta ni a fi n gba ile nigba ti a wa ni sanitation, ati awon eyan wa to si wa nibe. Sugbon awa ti won pin si ile iwe, lati ago meje ti a ba ti lo, o di ago meji ki a jade. Yato si igba ti ijoba tie ti wa gbe lesson kale bayi to je wipe o di ago merin. Amo a o tii ri nkankan gbo, salary OYES wa naa la n gba.

RF: we are praying God to please have mercy on us that were deployed to the schools. Those who work in the other sections such as sanitation work between 7 and 10am: we all swept the roads for only 3 hours while we were still in sanitation section, but those of us taken to the schools have to resume at 7am and close at 2pm. It has gotten even worse now that Government has introduced extra afternoon lesson which keeps us at work till 4pm. We have not seen any increase in the pay; we are still being paid the regular OYES stipend.

AS: salary OYES, 10 thousand ma niyen?

AS: OYES salary, that is 10 thousand naira?

RF: beeni

RF: yes

AS: sugbon awon to wa ni bi paramedics, to wa ni bii GMT, won ni salary awon gbe peli die ju ti OYES lo. Bawo ni tiyin se je?

AS: but those in the Paramedics and GMT say they get a monthly pay that is slightly higher than that of OYES

RF: awa naa gbo be, a de maan ri. Tori mo ti ri ninu circular ri ni ojo kan. O da bi pe awon kan wa be ti won ngba up to 15 thousand. Sugbon awa ni O' TEACHING o, 10 thousand la n gba.

RF: we also hear that and we also see it: I saw the circular once. It seems there are some that are paid as much as 15 thousand naira. However, we in O' TEACHERs, we are still paid 10 thousand naira.

AS: ti a ba ni ki e so iwoye yin nipa eto OYES, ki ni e ma so?

AS: if asked to give your opinion about OYES, what would that be?

RF: eto OYES, ni temi o, o je eto kan ti o daa to de tun tan ise ohun osi. Tori ti kii ba se be ni, o seese ko je wipe 10 thousand ti a n gba yi- a mo wipe, o bembe ko bembe, ati fi okan sipe ti osu ba pari a gba nkankan nibi ise ti a n se- sugbon to ba je wipe ijoba o gbe anfani yi kale fun wa ni ko si ibi ti aa lero e si: onikaluku wa na, bo se private school la le wa ni, bo se oja la le maa wa nkankan ta ni iwaju ile wa ni, ohun laa ba ma se. sugbon ope si ni fun Olohun lori an faani ti ijoba se fun awa odo ni ipnle osun tori ko je ki a maa rare kaakiri.

RF: OYES, in my opinion, is a very beneficial programme that remedies poverty. Without it, thths ere would not be any hope of getting paid, no matter how little, at the end of the month. We have hope that there is a 10 thousand somewhere. If Government had not made available this opportunity, each one of us would either have been trapped in some private schools or doing petty trades in our various homes. Thank God for the Government's initiative that has rescued the youth from hardship and lack.

AS: ti a ba ni ki e gba ijoba ni iyanju nipa eto OYES, kini ee so fun ijoba?

AS: if you have the chance to advice Government on the OYES, what would it be?

RF: ni temi o,maa koko dupe lowo ijoba ni: tori won ni ku ise lo n mu ise ya. Adupe lowo won gidigidi fun anfaani ti won fun wa. A si tun hu wa ki won tun bawa je ki nkan yi ko tun te siwaju, lati je wipe awa odo a o ni le maa rare kaakiri, tori Yoruba ni owo to ba dile ni esu n be lowe. Sugbon latari pe a n ji laaro a tie n ri nkankan se, inu wa na n dun ara wa de n ya. Mo dupe lowo ijoba. Ki won tun gbiyanju lati bawa gbon owo si awo eto yi. Ki won de ma je ko dawo duro sibe.

RF: personally, I should start by appreciating Government because they deserve all accolades. We really thank them for the opportunity given us. We would also like to encourage them to let it continue so that youths will not have to suffer in idleness. An idle mind is the devil's workshop. Having some form of positive engagement everyday gives one a sense of fulfillment. I thank Government. They should do more to ensure that the programme continues.

APPENDIX XII

AN INTERVIEW CONDUCTED WITH ALHAJI AKINGBOLA ILE-IFE, 28TH OCTOBER, 2016

WUMI RAJI

Assisted by
Folasade Adewale Lawal and Adetokunbo Shittu

WR: Good afternoon sir, Alhaji Akingbola. I am Wumi Raji. I teach in Obafemi Awolowo University, Ile-Ife. I am the one leading this research. With me are my research assistants: Mrs. Sade Adewale-Lawal and Mr. Tokunbo Shittu. We were told that you were the chairman of the Nigeria Union of Tailors, Osun State Chapter at the time that this project was started. Let me know how they first contacted you and how they got your data

ALH: Late in 2010, just a month and a half after Aregbesola came into office, I was sent for by some of our members in Osogbo. I went there and I was told that there was a job coming in that Aregbe wanted to give a contract of sewing to tailors in Osun State. They said they wanted people that could sew English dresses very well. One of our members who was very close to one of the lieutenants of Aregbe was contacted. He sent for me and took me to one Barrister Gbenga Akano. They asked me that, do you have registration certificate. I said we have. We have a registration certificate of Nigeria Union of Tailors and also that of the Cooperative CICU of Nigeria Union of Tailors. I took the two certificates to that man and he said that we are okay. He said he would be sending that certificate to Lagos. They were operating from Lagos as at then. So, we were called to Aregbe House

WR: Aregbe House, is it Government House?

ALH: Not Government House, that storey building

WR: Okay, that storey building, you mean the campaign office?

ALH: Yes. So we met some people like the Young… I can't remember their names.

WR: Kola Young. Kola Babatunde Young

ALH: Kola Young and some others; they were about 4 to 5 in number. We met together with my lieutenants. I think we were about 11 the day we met them. They interviewed us and showed us a sample of that OYES material that they have sewn in Lagos. They asked that if they gave that job to us, can we finish 500 pieces in 72 hours? We said we would. We negotiated, they told us to come back there again for sample. I mobilized the tailors at Osogbo because it can not be given out to people outside Osogbo so that people at Osogbo can sew that 500. And indeed, we finished that 500 pieces in record time. So, they appreciated what we've done.

WR: Maybe we should go back a bit by asking you to tell us a little about yourself. Maybe your background, your education, where you came from and, your training as a tailor; to make you become president.

ALH: I am Alhaji Kola Adegbola, native of Ife. This tailoring profession I inherited it from my father. I started learning this work from my father when I came back from school. I started school at Offa in 1947. I came back to Ife in 1949. My father told me that, look, I wouldn't like you to be playing ball around. Ijebu people if they are doing a certain job all their children must know about that job, so after leaving the school I should face this tailoring work. Which I did; I cooperated with him. I was learning the tailoring job alongside my education. So, when I passed out in 1956, the first set of primary 6- I am one of the first set of primary 6- so, I stayed at home for 2 or 3 years before I went to modern school in 1959 to 61. I had to train myself, I did part time grade III teacher's course and I became an auxiliary teacher. I did part time grade 2 which made me to become a qualified teacher.

WR: When you became a teacher. I also hold a Grade 2 certificate myself- of St. Andrew's college, Oyo

ALH: So I also did a year of Associateship course which I did at University of Ife here. I retired in the year 1998 as a teacher, a class teacher. I was doing the teaching service and tailoring. When I left school I came to my shop to do my work fully. It was in 1989 that I became the first president before the creation of Osun state. I was the first president

WR: 1989? You were still in service then

ALH: I was still in service. We wanted to register this union as Oyo State Tailors' Union but we were disappointed by Corporate Affairs Commission. They didn't register us in time. When they created Osun State, I told my members at Oyo Sate that if we happened to register Oyo and Osun, Okeogun or Ibadan State or whatever they are agitating for came in, they may be registering also in their name. I told them Nigeria Union of Teacher through out Nigeria is one. I told them if they can set a constitution and make it national in outlook they will register us. Any state created will only join the Nigerian Union of Tailors. It will be the umbrella union of tailors all over Nigeria. They agreed with me and they started processing that union. The certificate came out in 1994, July, so the year we started preaching the gospel of Nigeria Union of Tailors which we keep till now. It is only in the Eastern part of Nigeria that we don't have many members but we still have presence in some areas of that part of Nigeria. So, that was how we started. I was the first national president. I became the first national president in 1994

WR: The national president of Nigeria Union of Tailor?

ALH: I combined the two offices because the Oyo State's we were together. We were holding meetings in Oyo and Osun but Ibadan people abruptly broke that union. The association between us and Oyo we were doing it Oyo and Osun but when this Nigeria Union of Tailors came they said they will choose their own president so I organized that of Osun here then we broke up. I was holding that post till 2012 when I relinquished my office to Prince Akinloye in Ifon Osun.

WR: Thank you very much. You talked of 500 uniforms, was that all?

ALH: Not all. We were given 20 thousand pieces of that cloth. Along the line when we were given the job they took one quarter of it, they diverted it back to Lagos. The sample came from Lagos. When we discovered that they wanted to play another game with us we tried to struggle and check them and get it back. Out of that 20 thousand about one quarter was taken to Lagos. That three quarter of that 20 thousand is what we sewed for the OYES people.

WR: So, when you got that one, was it now through out…

ALH: When the job came, I called my members, because we have 30 and a half Local Governments in Osun State. I told them that this job given to us… I told them that ore Olohun enikan ki da aya bo. When we the officers explain that the informant was shot with an unregistered bullet shortly before they arrived the scene. Osun, the Local Government that is regular- at times we get 15 Local Government, at times we get 18 and at time we get 20. I tell them that if we spread this job to those who are not contributing to the union they may come back to play a better role than those who have been contributing to the union. They accepted. I said to the nook and corner of Osun State we should take it. So, that's how we spread that contract given to us to every Local Government, which they appreciated. And this job brings us together. If not because of this OYES uniform, when I wanted to leave, maybe I should have left the union to maybe 20 or 25 Local Governments because when Oyinlola gave us interest free loan I split that money to 30 Local Governments and anybody who didn't want it left their own in the bank. Some Local Governments didn't show up. But when this Aregbe job came in, the first one, they know what they realized and they are doing fine till now. This Aregbe contract brings us together and we plan together. From it we built a hall, tailors hall

WR: Where is it built?

ALH: Kelebe in Osogbo. It cost us about 7 million. It is the gain we realized from the contract given to us that we used in building the tailor's hall. It is what we gained from it and we cannot forget in time.

WR: There is one other organisation, Nigeria Society of Professional Tailors

ALH: NSPT… They emanated from Ibadan I think around 1990. There is one Collins. He was the one who organized that union. He is a big tailor: he has money; he established well and has so many apprentices. So for one reason or the other, he vied for chairmanship and failed, he vied for vice-chairmanship and failed, he vied for treasurer he failed, so just organized it. So they are very minute. They are just a dissident group that doesn't …when this Aregbe contract came in, those NSPT were trying to come up as a body but were directed to come and meet the Nigeria Union of Tailors, they've won the contract. I told my members tailor is tailor. Ore Olohun enikan kii da aya bo. We gave them a reasonable percentage of the job and when they wanted to deliver the share given to them, they brought it to me; I packed it together as a body and delivered it to those who are in charge of the thing.

WR: How were you paid because it looks like, from what you have said now, there was no dilly-dallying on the part of the Government in paying for what you have done? Is it before, during or after?

ALH: When we started they mobilized us with 10 million…so when we finished the job and delivered they paid us the balance.

WR: So, you said that the tailors all benefited from it and even built a hall from it. What about personal gain…personal benefits and all that for the individual tailors?

ALH: The individual tailors, we paid them for the work given to them.

WR: Were they all able to do something from it individually?

ALH: I cannot say because, in Ife Central here, I coordinated Ife Central, Ife East and Area Office. If the material came here I distributed to every Local Government. if every local government had to sew about 100, they will bring it, we will pack it and take it down. Because of what we gave to them, when the money came in it is on this table that we share so that everybody got. I am talking of Ife Zone; this is where everybody got … how many cloths did you sew? …so we distributed the money. When they get to their Local Government those who worked on it will be paid. I can't say the individual gain. I don't know what they have done with it. But there is nobody that will say that he worked but didn't get paid.

WR: And they all were satisfied…happy with it?

ALH: They cooperated with the union more than before. They stood firmly as members till today. It is that job that waxed us together.

WR: Thank you very much. What general comment do you have on OYES as a project? How do you see it as a project?

ALH: It is a good way of empowerment for the young people and the tailors…whether you are young or not you are empowered. We really appreciate it. That is the reason why we showed appreciation to Aregbe sometime in 2013 at Mandela Park.

WR: How did you do this? How did you show the appreciation and what exactly did you do?

ALH: That Mandela Park, we rented that place 100 thousand Naira. We invited him together with his co-workers. We organized a very elaborate programme to show that we are very grateful to him. We really appreciated him. It was a full day programme. He himself came, and his other lieutenants. They came and they appreciated it. We organized some cultural people to dance…a lot of programme was there which he really appreciated and knew that we are grateful for what he has done. So, personally I appreciate Aregbe for employing 20 thousand youths. Instead of giving cutlasses to people to be touts and thugs …what he did, the cutlass seller, the rake seller…that is used for clearing the road. Most of the artisans and traders know that there were changes in their lives when Aregbe came. The sign writers and artists…also can't forget him for the jobs given to them. All artisans generally know that there was change

WR: If you are to advise government…Osun State government about the programme, what will you say that they should do or not do? Your free advice

ALH: If I will advise the government on what they have done to see that people are not jobless, I will advise him to set up vocational training centres. If he can establish vocational training centres and ask people to apply...because if you have interest in something you will be able to do it well than the one you are forced to do which you don't have interest in. I think during the western region Awolowo did something. He established weaving centre and the ceramic centre... anything pertaining to hand work ...even tailoring. I think they have done that but it is his own personal business.

WR: Aregbesola?

ALH: Aregbesola. That Omoluabi Garment Factory is his own personal business...

WR: The one in Osogbo?

ALH: Yes, the one in Osogbo. So, he can collect people... I will advise them they can expand that trade centre; they will have tailoring section, electrical something. It was on before. They should try to make sure that they start that again and put money into that trade centre for people to learn trade of their interest. That's what I think can help the youth than white collar job. That trade centre is the main something. They can be learning photography in the trade centre. Series of hand work ...

WR: thank you very much; I don't know if anyone has a question

AS: On the NUT, what are the criteria for joining your association?

ALH: Joining the association...let's say I am your apprentice, the day I am obtaining freedom from you the master tailors will be on seat. They will pray for me, they will advise me from what they've experienced. Let's say you are my master, you will call your master tailors too and they will be advising me, this is way to go, this is how to deal with customers...so, the day you are obtaining your freedom, there is no any other word, the particulars that are given to you ...the consent certificate, I have become a member. I will be co-operating with whatever the union wants... So, there is no other ...

SAL: Is it possible for me to say I want to join the NSPT even if I first belong to the NUT?

ALH: There is freedom of everything: freedom of religion, freedom of association....

WR: It's been a pleasure talking to you Alhaji. We thank you very much.

ALH: Thank you too.

APPENDIX XIII

INTERVIEW WITH ALH. MUSIBAU A. ISOLA AND MR. WAKILI ISOLA ON 1ST FEBRUARY, 2017

WUMI RAJI

Assisted by Adetokunbo Adeola Shittu

WR: e kaasan o, Alhaji. Inu wa dun pe a pe yin e je wa. A dupe ni owo yin. omowe Ajewumi Raji ni oruko temi. Obafemi Awolowo university nibi ni mo tin sise olukoni. Adetokunbo Shittu ni oruko oluranlowo mi lori ise yi…eniketa wa ti o le wa, iya aafin Adewale Lawal ni oruko ti e… inu wa a dun ti e ba le salaye fun wa nipa ara yin; oruko yin ati ibi ti e ti wa ati ise ti e n se

WR: Good afternoon, Alhaji. We are elated to see that you honored our request to have this interview with you. My name is Dr. Ajewumi Raji. I work here at the Obafemi Awolowo University. My assistant is Adetokunbo Shittu…the third person, who is unavoidably absent, is Mrs. Adewale Lawal. We will be happy if you tell us about yourself: your name, your place of origin and occupation

AI: Oruko temi ni Musibau A. Isola, oludasile ile ise BRIMAC INDUSTRIES, ti a n pe ni MUSI SHOES. Musibau yen lo duro fun MUSI SHOES. Mo da ile ise yen le ni bi ogun odun ati odun mejo, 28 years. Mo de ti wa lenu e ko to di pe mo da ile ise yen sile

AI: My name is Musibau A. Isola, Chairman of BRIMAC INDUSTRIES, also know as MUSI SHOES, which is a coinage from the name Musibau. I established the company about 28 years ago and I have been involved with shoes long before its establishment.

WR: e ti wa lenu ise bata sise?

WR: You have been involved in shoe making?

AI: beeni. Mo bere sii lo si ilu oyinbo bi 1976

AI: Yes. I started travelling overseas around 1976

WR: nibo gangan ni ilu oyinbo?

WR: Where exactly did you visit overseas?

AI: Italy. Mo ni ore kan ni be. 77 ni mo koko lo but mi o ri. Mo tun pada. 78 ni mo wa lo; so mo maan lo bi every two months or three months. Nigba ti ilu si daa, papa gaan mo ma n lo larin ose meji; ti maa poyi lee meji. Nigba yen mo n ko bata wa, mo n ko shirts wa. Gbogbo e ni mo n se: karakata. Mo wa wo pe, ma sa dagba lojo kan. Ki emi na tie da nkan le si ilu mi. enikan wa ti a n pe ni baba Limson, o wu mi ki ni oruko bi baba yen se loruko nigba yen; 60s ni baba yen ti n se bata. Won n pe ni Alimi. O n je LIMSON SHOES. mo wa wo pe emi naa fe loruko, ni mo fida ile ise yen sile nigba yen. Mo gba awon oyinbo kan. (to Mr. Wakili)Osu melo ni won fi ba wa sise na?

AI: Italy. I had a friend there. I first visited in '77 but could not locate him, so I went again in '78. After then I visited at 2 or 3 months' intervals. When the economy was still buoyant, there were times I went and returned like twice within two weeks. At that time, I imported shoes and shirts. I did general merchandising. At some point I thought to myself that I was not getting any younger, it was time I established something in my home country. There was a man we called LIMSON. I wished to be famous like him; he had started making shoes since the 60's. His name was Alimi. His brand was LIMSON SHOES. I wanted to be famous too so I started the company then. I had some white men working for me. (to Mr. Wakili) How many months did we have them working with us?

WI: osu bi meta

WI: About 3 months

AI: ni won fiba mi sise ni igba yen, won to pada si ilu won nigba ti a ti mo owo nkan ti a nse tan. Koto di pe mo da ile ise sile, mo ti n wa ile. Nigba ti a ko tan, a ko ni iko ile ise gaan. Photo e nisin yi, ma fi han yin. o tobi. O je bi 200 by 180 meters. Bi ware house gaan ni. awon OYES fe se bata, mo ba lo bawon…

AI: They worked with me then until we mastered the craft ourselves and they went back to their country. Before I established the factory, I was scouting for a favourable location and when we eventually built it, we made it a full fledged factory. I will show you the pictures of it shortly. It is quite large spanning about 200 by 180 meters. It is like a warehouse. The OYES wanted to make boots so I went to see them

WR: e seun, ki a to de ibe yen. Ile ise yin yi, se o si n se ise ni gbogbo igba yen; e si n fi se bata titi di igba ti awon OYES?

WR: Thank you. Before we get there: this factory of yours, was it still operational when OYES started?

AI: an se ise sugbon ko dabi. Idi nipe bata China ko je ki a ta mo. Sebi mo n sise fun Bata

AI: It was running but not at full capacity because imported Chinese foot wears have taken over our market. I was working for bata, initially.

WR: e n se bata ti e n supply won?

WR: you made shoes and supplied Bata?

AI: in fact, MD won wa si odo mi, Production Manager won wa si odo mi ni factory yen ni Iwo. igba ti o wa ya, a maan se meeting ni Manufacturers Association, ti a n se meeting, ki ni a fe se soro yi? Government policy o help wa. Bata ti o n wole lati china igbamiin o maan le ni 1o million. iru aso yi, synthetic ni ti won kan kun loda. Aso ni, won kan kun loda ni. after odun kan a bere si ni ma ate puke. Won wa so pe won fe se OYES. Engineer Rauf Aregbesola fe ki awon eeyan ni ise lowo; ki gbogbo awon eeyan ni advantage ninu ijoba e. o gbe ise sita fun wa. Mo mun sample lo. Mo poyi ibe to bi osu meta ko to diipe mo ri ise yen gba

AI: In fact, their MD came to my factory, and the Production Manager too visited our factory at Iwo. At some point we held meetings at Manufacturers' Association to find a solution to the problem but Government's policies are ever unfavorable. Shoes imported from China sometime can be up to the tune of 10 million pairs. Fabrics such as this are synthetically quoted. This begins to break after a year. When they came up with OYES, Engr. Rauf Aregbesola simply wanted to give people employment to enable them feel the impact of Government. He awarded us the contract, I presented a sample. I followed up the contract for about 3 months before I got it.

WR: odun wo niyen? Ohun ti a gbo ni wipe ni gba ti won koko bere, Aba ni won ti lo ko eyi ti won koko se wa

WR: What year was that? We learnt that when the scheme started, the first batch of boots was ordered from Aba

AI: looto ni. o tie di wahala siwon lorun ti won sope awon Bokoharam ni won se bata fun… ni 2013

AI: That is true. It really became a big trouble when it was alleged that they made the boots for Boko Haram, in 2013

WR: okay, second batch ni tiyin?

WR: Obviously, you got the second batch

AI: won wa wo ile ise wa

AI: They came to inspect the factory

WR: won wa wo ile ise yin nigba ti e lo so fun won pe a n se nkan bayi o?

WR: They came to inspect your factory when you went to notify them of what you do?

AI: won de wa pelu commandante won. Won sa to awon merin. Foto won wa nbi ti a ya nigba na

AI: And they came along with the commandante. There were four of them. We have the photographs of the visit

WR: a le wo won but awon ti a maa mo ni: boya bi mr. odulaja wa nbe, commandante wa nbe, kola young wa nbe

WR: We will see the pictures, I am sure they are all familiar faces like Mr. Odulaja, Commandante and Kola Young

AI: won wa nbe

AI: They were all present

WR: awon to gbe ise fun wa niyen

WR: Those are the ones who gave us this contract

AI: gbogbo won na lo wa nibe. A jo ya foto na nbe. Won rin kiri ni ile ise yen, won ni o wa okay; won ni awon a gbe ise fun wa. Won tie ni ti awon ba gbe ise fun wa ta o ba se, won ni awon a fi olopa mu wa

AI: They were all there and we took a picture together. They toured the facility and affirmed it was okay. They promised to award us the contract. They even threatened to get us arrested should we fail to execute the project

WR: bi won se so fun emi naa niyen: pe ti a ba gbe ise yi fun e, ti a fun e lowo, ti oo ba se…

WR: That was exactly what I was told too: that if they gave me the contract and I failed to do it…

AI: awon o fi olopa mu wa. Nigba to ya won gbe ise yen fun wa. Won ni ki a lo gba bank guarantee wa, a de lo gba bank guarantee fun won . won fun wa lowo an ba ise lo. Ti won ba ti fun wa an supply won ni Asiko ti a ba da. won de gbe egberun marun fun wa. Ile ise wa n se bata, to ba je on full capacity, a maan se bata egberun meta lojumo. Nkan to sele nipe by the time ti won gbe fun wa a ti reduce awon osise wa, eyan o kan le maa sanwo lasan. Won ni cut your coat according to your size. A ri wipe nkan ti a ba le se. nigba ti o ya a wa so awon kan di bi ki eeyan gba temporary staff abi contract staff; ti won ba se mejo bayi, a o san owo mejo fun won. Tori ti a o ba ni ise lowo, ti a ba gba won a o maa san owo osu won lo. Sugbon to ba je contract ni

AI: That they were going to call the police to arrest us. They later gave us the contract. They said we should present a bank guarantee, which we presented. We got paid and commenced work. Each batch we got, we completed and returned on schedule. They gave us 5000 pairs. Our factory, when working at full capacity, could produce 3000 pairs of shoes in a day. However, by the time we got the contract we had reduced our work force; we simply could not continue to pay them for nothing. We later converted some to contract staff and paid them on the bases of the quantity of work they do. That was necessary in order not to continue to incur expenses while there was not work to do.

WR: ti ise ba ti tan enikaluku a maa lo

WR: So, everyone went away once the contract was completed?

AI: nigba ti a nise gaan ni won to wa o. a ni permanent staff; koda a ni quarters fun won. Ise n lo deede nigba yen. Sugbon nigba to ya ti Chinese bere sini ko bata wole lo di boo lo o ya nmi. Ni gbogbo e wa daru. Emi ni Bata, won o rise se mo. Gbogbo shoe industry; a mo'ra wa. A de so fun won pe ise ti e fe gbe sita yi a le se gbogbo e ti won ba le fun wa. Won de so pe awon maa pin fun gbogbo awon ti won n se bata inu ile; alafowose se.

AI: They resumed when we got the contract. We used to have permanent staff and a staff quarters. Then work progressed steadily. Things became bad when the Chinese began to import their products. All the shoe manufacturers went out of business. We the shoe business organisations knew one another quite well. We informed Government that our company has the capacity to handle the entire project but they insisted on sharing it to accommodate the small scale and petty shoe makers.

WR: in fact a ti n interview awon iyen na. igba ti mo n ba yin soro yen mo ro pe ko yato sira. E o ripe mo n so fun yin pe a ma wa ko to dipe e so fun mi pe e o gbe motor wa. Igba ti mo to ri yin ati moto yin ni mo to mo pe o yato sira. A lo interview baba kan ni Osogbo

WR: We have actually interviewed some of those too. I can see the similarity in your opinion to theirs. You will notice that the initial arrangement was for us to visit you before you insisted on driving down. It was until I saw you with your car that I saw that you are on a different level. We had an interview with an elderly shoe maker in Osogbo the other day

AS: Alhaji Ganiyu ni Oke Baale l'osogbo

AS: Alhaji Ganiyu at Oke Baale, Osogbo

AI: abe ile lawon wa

AI: He operates on a very small scale

WR: awon alabe ile, bi nkan ti e so. won pin kaakiri ni pe ki onikaluku le je nbe

WR: You are right. The contract was equitably shared out so that everyone could benefit from it

AI: a o oppose iyen but iyato ma n wa ninu nkan ti eeyan ba fi irinse se gidi. Irinse po lori ba. Bata de ni 16 components. 16 components ni bata ni. kiise awo lasa. O lowu, o ni gum. Gum e pe orisi meta. O ni toe board, oni back canter, o ni shank…different items to wa ninu bata. Ka sa ma fa orogun sa, won sa gbe ise yen fun wa, a de se. won de fun wa ni owo wa lasiko

AI: We are not opposed to that but there is always a huge difference between what is mechanically manufactured and that which is done manually; whereas a normal shoe has 16 components apart from leather. We use yarns, gums: three different kinds of gum, toe board, back canter, and shank…different items that a shoe comprises of. Anyway, we got the contract, did it and got paid without delay.

WR: nigba ti won gbe ise yen fun yin, se won da igba ti o ye ki e da pada?

WR: Were you given a deadline for completion of the contract when it was awarded?

AI: won so fun wa

AI: Yes, we were

WR: o to igba wo; se ose kan ni, abi osu kan abi osu meji?

WR: how long: a week, a month or two months?

AI: igba ti won koko gbe fun wa na, won ni awon need ikan urgent, won fun wa ni 3 weeks and ki ojo yen to pe ati submit e fun won

AI: the first batch we got was to be completed and returned urgently. We had just 3 weeks to submit and we had completed the work and given it to them long before that ultimatum.

WR: leyin igba yen ni won wa tun gbe imiin fun yin?

WR: then you got another one?

AI: won tun wa gbe immin fun wa

AI: they gave us another batch thereafter

WR: leyin igba ti won gbe ise yi fun yin, se won sanwo die fun yin ni?

WR: after you were awarded the contract, were you paid in part or in full?

AI: won san owo die fun wa

AI: we got part payment

WR: ki e to bere ise? Igba ti e wa pari nko?

WR: before you started work? And when you completed it?

AI: won san owo iyoku

AI: they paid the balance

WR: ko si pe? Ko si fitina?

WR: without delay and hassles?

AI: ko si

AI: not at all

WR: awon naa nko?

WR: what about them? Did they keep their part of the bargain?

AI: awon na o fi owo wa dun wa o. won te wa lorun gaan. Won o fi nkankan je wa niya

AI: they did not fail on paying the balance on time. In fact, we were impressed. They did not fail on providing us with all we needed

WR: ise yi, bawo lo se ri? E mo pe igba miin wa ti eeyan o gba ise miin ti eyan o so pe ise yi bawo lo se ri yii?

WR: and how do you assess the project? You know, there are times when one gets such a project and one does not in the least break even. Did you find this profitable?

AI: inu mi dun fun oro ti e so yen. Nkan ti o ba ise wa je, awa o le se. orisirisi awo lo wa o. a ri awon ti won fi owo tan, a ri awon ti won fi machine tan. Grade by grade ni awo. O dun mi pe won fun wa ni sample. Nkan ti won fun wa ni a se fun won. E ma je ki n soro lo si odo awon ikeji wa ti won gba ise, aa da bi pe mo n ba won je. Awa o le compromise pelu quality wa. Ki won wa so pe igba ti won se tan bata won de n si. Awa o le se. so, ise ti won fun wa, ere ti a ri nbe ki Olorun fi alubarika si. But to ba se pe a fe gba lodo won ka se dada…o keep ile ise wa busy nigba yen na. awon kan de tun sise nbe to sepe awon ri tiwon naa nbe. Tori eni ti e pe ko wa sise,to gba owo e lasiko, yi o maa sadua fun yin ni. so, nigba yen, awon omo Iwo wa…awon na jere oselu

AI: I am quite pleased with that statement. We can not compromise on quality. There are different types of leather. There are those that are tanned manually and there are those done mechanically. It was unfortunate that we were given a sample. It was based on that sample that we produced. I need not digress talking about our competitors lest I begin to sound like I am trying to damage them. We never compromise on our quality. It can not be said that the shoes we built were not durable. We can not do that. We are truly contented with the profit we made from what we were awarded. But if we had been enabled to make the shoes to our own standard… meanwhile, the contract kept our company engaged and those who worked with us made some profits too. Of course, everyone who is invited to work and is paid on time will be grateful for such an opportunity. Indigenes of Iwo got work with us and, indirectly, enjoyed the dividend of democracy

WR: se e mo pe awon oloselu, nkan ti won maan saba se ni pe ki won gba won fun…body guard, igba miin wa ti won a so pe, boya 50 thousand tabi 20 thousand, agbole yi e gba, supporter wa. Ni orisirisi ona ti oloselu fi maan gbayan sise, ona ti won fi maan se anfani fun ilu

WR: the politicians, if you observe, have the habit of engaging youths as bodyguards, on some other occasions, they give handouts of about 50 thousand or 20 thousand naira to some clusters of supporters… the several ways that politicians give people employment to benefit society

AI: a je mudunmudun ijoba tiwantiwa lasiko igba ti Aregbe wa nibe

AI: we enjoy the dividend of democracy during the tenure of Aregbesola

WR: nkan ti mo wan so nipe mudunmudun yi, orisirisi ona lo le gba wa

WR: what I am saying exactly is that dividends of democracy come in various forms

AI: mudunmudun pe won gbe ise fun wa ni o

AI: the dividend I mean relates only to the contract we were awarded

WR: nkan ti mo n so niyen. Mudunmudun yi ti e ba fi we iyoku

WR: that is the point I am trying to make. Can you compare that dividend or benefit to anything previously obtainable?

AI: ko le dabi. Se e ri, lowo ti a wa nisinyi, nipa oro ise yi nsiyi, eni to ba fe ri ise gidi gba nisinyi afi odo ijoba to ri awon eeyan o lagbara lati ra nkan mo. Ko si owo nita. Emi nsinyi mo n wa ise kaakiri nsinyi. Mo ti gba ise olopa ri, mo ti gba ise prison ri, mo ti gba ise immigration. Mo tun n pada lo ibe. A o le se bata nsinyi ka ni a fe ta; o won. Tori awo nsinyi ti won. Ti a ba ni a ko sita pe e wa ra, won o ni ra tori, gbese lo ma je. But ijoba. Eni ti o ti jeun, se o f era bata ni

AI: not at all. Presently, anyone who wishes to get a good job or contract looks up to the government because the people are fast losing purchasing power. There is poverty in the land. I, for instance, have to run from pillar to poles to get contracts. I have worked for the police, the prison service and the immigration. I still plan to go back there. We can not produce for the masses because the cost of production is high and the products expensive. If we produce and put it out in the market for sale, we would not be able to break even. How can one expect a hungry man to buy shoes?

WR: nkan ti e n so ni sinyi ni pe o daa ki ijoba maa gbe ise jade ju ki won maa fun

WR: what you are saying, if I understand, is that Government should issue contracts rather than give handouts?

AI: awon eeyan ni torokobo lo

AI: yes

WR: kini ohun ti e wa ri si oro OYES yen; yato si wipe won gbe ise fun yin, pe e de se, e de gbe pada fun won. OYES gangan funra re ti won se bata yi fun, Programme yen, kin ni nkan ti e ri so si?

WR: what is your opinion about OYES; besides the fact that you were awarded a contract, and you executed and delivered it on time, what do you think about the scheme for which you built the boots?

AI: ibeere ti e beere yen daa pupo o. se e ri awon ti o ri ise se ti won gba si ise nigba yen, ti e ba n lo ni titi, e o maa ri ti won o maa san oko lo. Opolopo lo n se adura fun won lasiko yen. Yato si wipe awa gaan sise fun won, ti emi gan ba ri ti won n san oko lo ni titi bayi, at least won ti e n ri nkan mu lo ile losu, o daa pupo. Nkan ti a fe ki ijoba se niyen. Ki awon eeyan ni ise lowo ki won ri ise se. kii se pe ki won kan maa fun won ni owo; gba 20 thousand, baba rankadede! Ki won gbe ise sita. Iru eyi ti won se yen; ti OYES se yen nsiinyi, a mo pe o na won lowo o, but mekunu mi ti o ri ise se, won n ri ise se. boya sile kan ni won ba mu lo ile, iyawo o je n be, omo o je n be. Ere lo je nigba yen fun opolopo. Emi naa ni woman kan ni ile mi, ibe lo ti n sise

AI: That was a good question. Youths who were unemployed hitherto were engaged; you will see them cutting road verges vigorously. A lot of people are pleased with this. Apart from the contract I got, each time I see the youths at work, I am elated because it is a means of enabling them earn a pay at the end of the month. That is what we want Government to do; to provide employment for people. That is more beneficial than giving people handouts of 20 thousand Naira, making praise singers of the masses. Although the OYES is capital intensive, it provided job for the common folks. They are able to provide for their families from what money they earn from there. I actually have a woman in my neighborhood who was engaged in OYES

WI: iyawo Doctor. Ibe lo gbe achieve ise tie

WI: the Doctor's wife. She was able to start up her own business from the monthly allowance

AI: owo to ri gba nibe lo fi da ise tie naa sile

AI: she started the business from her savings while working in the scheme

WR: iru ise wo lo da sile nigba yen?

WR: what sort of business did she start up?

WI: o n ta awon ate; bi ka ta minetrals, ka ta nkankan

WI: groceries and household provisions like soft drinks

AI: so owo to rigba ninu OYES nigba yen

AI: so, she was able to do that with her OYES allowance

WI: o ti improve awon omo e. ko siipe oko fee de, yi o ban wa silekan. Nigba ti oun na tile wo OYES, ti o ti n gba torokobo. Ninu awon ohun to n daa jo lo fi bere owo tie. Ninu won, awon to je graduates wontibe bo sibi ise won. To ba je pe Doctor ni, won o fi si enu ise tie, yio ma ba doctor lo. Eni to ba je teacher, won o fi si enu ibi teacher tie, yio ma ba tie lo. Won n gba ona OYES yen, awon to ba ni qualification lowo, won n gba ona ibeyen lati ri ise to jemo ise tiwon

WI: she has been able to provide for her children. She no longer has to wait on her husband to get a lot of things done since she got some money saved from OYES work. Some cadets who were graduates also got employed to better positions as Doctors and teachers through the exit programme arrangement. Those who have good qualifications get better jobs through the OYES

AI: lafikun, iranlowo lo je fun awon mekunu. Woni ti orikan ba suwon a ran igba. By the time to gbe ise yen fun wa, awon to je labe tiwa naa po. Nigba ti a gba ise yen, awon kan naa je nbe lo: awon to supply materials, awon ti a gba losise, awon naa ri ere nibe. Awon ti o ta ohunje. O fi ran ilu lowo

AI: in addition, it was of great benefit to the masses. When we got the contract a lot of people benefited from it. Those who supplied the materials and those whom we employed to assist with the production gained a lot; and the food vendors too. It eased the economic difficulty in the state

WR: eyi ti won wa n ro pe awon si tun fe gba 20 thousand miin, eyin ro pe ti won ba se, o da,bi irin ajo wa ti e tun fe so pe ki won rin?

WR: now they are planning to recruit another 20 thousand, do you feel it is the right thing to do; or you have a better suggestion?

AI: akoko na, yato fun to do wa, awon ti o je nbe lo maa po ti ilu o si tun dun. Nigba ti eyan o ba ri ise se, won ni owo to ba dile ni esu n be lowe. Ise o tun wa. Owo ti won ba tun wa ri nbe, elomiin a re jo. Elomiin a gba ominira ara e. ilu de tun n mo. Ilu yato. E o ri pe gbogbo bi won se n sanko yen, o n yato. O n tun ilu se awon eyan de tun je anfani e

AI: apart from our prospect, many will benefit from it and life will be easier for all. An idle mind, they say, is the devil's workshop. It will provide employment. People can save up the allowance and become self-reliant. You will observe that the state is cleaner due to their works. People are benefitting a lot from it

WR: e seun. E ti so nisinyi pe eyin naa mo pe orisirisi eyan ni won gbe ise bata yen fun. A si ti n ba awon tibi yen naa soro bi a se n ba yin soro yi; tori a o gbodo paro. Eyin ti e si ni e je bi big man ninu awon onibata ti a ti n ba soro; Iru iyanju wo ni e fe gba ijoba pe ti won ba fe gbe ise bata jade gege bi eni ti oni experience to de mo nipa ise yi?

WR: thank you so much. You have stated already that the contract was shared to all and sundry; and we have interviewed some of the other contractors, as a better established shoe manufacturer out of the lot, what, considering your level of experience in the business, is your advice to Government in case they want to give out such contracts in the future?

AI: e se, Olohun o ran yin lowo. Se eri, Ijoba, nkan ti won o se ni won ose; e o baa fun won ni imoran lati oni d'ola. Emi kan fe gba ni imoran pe ti won ba fe gbe ise sita ki won gbe ise sita sugbon ko je nti won a ri lo; ti a ni alope. Tori ti won ba gbe be, a ni igba ti won a lo. Kii se pe ki won ra bata loni ki sole gba ona Ibadan lo ki ori e gba ona ibo miin lo. Awon ti won ba gba na, ki won so fun won pe ti bata e o bad a, a o ni gba o. ti won ba de se be, awon ti won ba gba na, inu awon na a dun. Awon ti won o ri ise se lo poju ti won a tun rise se. koda, Aregbesola, to ba kuro nibe won o tun maa se adua fun. Tori awa o le sepe fun bayi tori nigba ti o gbe ise fun wa a ri torokobo nibe. Boti e se pe ko po, a ri nkankan nbe. Awomn ti won de bawa sise na, awon na ri nkankan nbe.

AI: thank you… actually; Government will only do what it has planned to do no matter what advice you proffer. Regardless of that, my advice is that durability should be their primary concern when giving out such contracts in the future. It is fruitless if the shoes begin to fall to pieces after brief usage. They should also endeavor to warn the contractors that poorly done work will not be accepted. That way, the Governor himself will incur blessings from the people after his tenure of office. Of course we cannot say negative things about him because we have benefitted from the work we did for him; even though it was not much. And those who assisted in the actual execution also profited.

WI: awon ti won o tun ko ise lodo wa na o wa ninu awon ti a ba gba. Awon na o tun lo da tiwon le nibo miin. Nkan ti a ba si fi lele fun won ni awon na o maa lo lo lohun.

WI: some of our employees will also have the opportunity of learning the craft on the job. They can go afterwards to establish their own business and continue to practise on the standard at which we have tutored them

WR: e je kin bere question kan to delicate, ti e ba ni e o fe dahun e, a o ni binu. Se e ri awon apere bata ti awon miin se to se pe o ku die kaato?

WR: let me ask this delicate question; you have every right not to answer it. Have you ever come across any such poorly produced boots, out of those previously done, that have so fallen to pieces?

AI: mi o ni le so nkankan lori iyen. E ma binu o

AI: I would rather not say anything on that. I am sorry

WI: eyan o gbodo ma tu asiri enikeji e

WI: It is wrong to reveal one's rivals' secrets

AI: inu mi ni mo mo, mi o mo inu elomiin. Ko ye ki a ma ba oja enikeji je. O sese bere ni. oun na o ma kogbon si.

AI: I only know about my own products. We should not run down the rival's effort. They just started off, they will learn on the job

AS: sir, mo discover pe large scale manufacturer ni yin

AS: Sir, I observe that you are a large scale manufacturer

AI: medium

AI: Medium

AS: medium, e o kii se abele, e wa well established. Kini nkan ti e ro pe ijoba le se fun awon ti o je OYES members to ni ife si ise owo kiko; yato si awon to je graduates?

AS: You are not operating on a small scale, you are well established. What do you think Government can do for those non-graduate OYES cadet members who have interest in technical training?

WR: iru awon ti o fe ko ise bi tiyin tabi nkan miin?

WR: Those who are interested in works like yours?

AI: ibere yen da pupo. Teletele emi na ti fe se institute of fashion or shoes, to sepe ti awon eyan ba a ma resume bi ti school to sepe ti won ba jade awon na ma wa self employed lai je pe won lo ba eyan. Ti Osun State ba le se be; even lodo wa nibeyen, iru odo wa ti won ba le ni, awon eyan ti n gba ibibayi wole o, e o ma train awon eyan o, inu mi a dun

AI: That is a good question. I already have the mind of starting up an institute of fashion or shoes, that will run normal training courses like a normal school so that graduands from there can be self-employed. If Osun State can do such, even if they come to seek our partnership on it, we shall willingly train them and that shall be with all pleasure

WR: eyin se tan lati offer iru training be ti ijoba ba se?

WR: You mean you are ready to offer such a training if Government initiates the move?

AI: bee ni

AI: Yes

AS: imiin ti mo tun fe bere ni, ti a ba fi oju sunnunkun wo, ti awon eyan ba join OYES, exit programme won, bi ki won lo si GMT, ki won lo si OAMBULANCE. Sugbon a ri wipe ni ibeyen, wo si ni lati duro de oye ti ijoba ba fun won ni ipari osu, to sepe ni iwoye temi, o ku die kaato. Ki ni eyin rope ijoba le se nipa idagbasoke ise owo?

AS: I have another but related question: on closer observation, one sees that OYES has in place exit programmes which deployed people to sections such as GMT and O'AMBULANCE; thereby enlisting them on a monthly pay scale. In my view, that does not really liberate them from dependence on financial confinement, which is inadequate. What do you think Government can do to boost growth in technical skills?

AI: se e ri, idagbasoke ise owo daa but ko si owo nilu. Ti owo ba wa ni idagbasoke seese, sugbon ti ko ba si owo ninu ko si nkan ti e fe se. lasiko yi o, ko si owo. O wa le di ola ko yi pada o. ni isin yi bayi, ati jeun elomiin paapa boya ekan lojumo ni. tori ilu dun ti ao gbodo so nkan miin. Ijoba naa fe se opolopo nkan sugbon igba ti ko ba si owo. Ni Osun paapa, koi ti yan commissioner tori ko si owo ni. iru eyi ti o fe se paapa, eyi ti e ni o fe se, tori ibi pakaleke naa ni

AI: The boost in that sector is a perfect idea but there is paucity of funds. It is only when funds are available that development is possible. Any meaningful growth in the technical skills can only be projected to happen in the future not now when people can hardly feed themselves. Government wishes to do a lot of things but there is insolvency presently. In Osun State presently, the Governor has not been able to appoint commissioners because there is no money to do so. His planned revival of the OYES at this time is even being done from the meager resources available.

WI: ibi pakaleke lahun gbee gberi

WI: it is not being done out of sheer convenience

AI: ibi pe ko si na lo ti fe mu owo jade lati fi dun awon eyan ninu. O fe dun awon eyan ninu ni o. kiise pe o fe…o ti yo n tie ti a ba kan n tan arawa je ni. nkan ti o fe se yi nsiyi o fe dun awon eyan ninu ni. pe, ah, iwo tie maa lo sise ntie. Bo wo ibe laago mejo to kuro nibe ni laago meta, at least ni ipari osu yi o gba owo kan. Owo yen o ran nkankan ninu idile to ti jade. Emi ro pe ki o se tori pe yio fun awon eyan lounje.

AI: It is from the little available resources that he will finance the project so as to alleviate people's suffering. He is doing it simply to help the people. He has all he would ever dream of already unless we are not being sincere to ourselves. He wants once again to get people to work. If they resume at 8:00am and close at 3:00pm, it is certain that they will have some money to take home at the end of the month. That money should solve some problems within the home. I think he should go ahead with the plan as it will alleviate people's suffering.

WR: ti won ba wa ki e gba ijoba ni imoran lori gbogbo nkan ti o n se, ki ni e ma so?

WR: What then is your advice to Government concerning its various projects?

AI: imoran ti mo ma gba nipe Olohun o fun se. n o ni ko se OYES miin; temi o je, ti awon elomiin na o je. Emi nikan ko ni mo ma je. Tori temi ba gba ise yen nisinyi, awon kan ni o se. won o le sepe. Awon kan na ni o da sita, awon na o ni sepe. Inu awon ara ilu o tun dun ni tori bi o se maa gba through out the whole Osun ni. yi o kari gbogbo Osun. Ti won ba si gbe bata fun wa na, awon to je enikeji wa na, awon na a jenbe won o ni sepe

AI: May God continue to help him. I will advise that he goes ahead with the OYES so that we can all benefit from it. If I get a contract there from, I should employ workers to get the job done. They surely will be happy working. Even the cadet members will be happy about it. The populace too will be glad because the scheme cuts across the entire state. When the shoe contracts are awarded we as well as our competitors will be positively affected.

WR: mo tie fe beere; eyin o si ninu…tori baba…Ganiyu, won so fun wa pe awon ni egbe onibata; Asiko yen awon de ra ile kan si ibikan ti awon si bere sini ko ile egbe. Won ni awon o tii pari e. eyin o si ninu egbe won?

WR: I should like to ask this; Elder Ganiyu informed us that there is an Association of Shoe Makers, who were able to acquire a piece of land and started work on the association's hall from proceeds of the previous OYES contracts. He said it was still under construction. Are you not a member of that association?

AI: mi o si ninu egbe won but mo wa ninu Manufacturers Association. About 27 years ni mo ti wa nibe. A ni ija pelu government nisinyi. Won gbe ise kan ni 250 million, 50 thousand pairs fun awon ara Aba. Won o de ni irin ise. Awa ti a wa ninu MAN, a wa sope, Government mo awon to ni shoe industry, ki lo de ti won o gbe fun won? For your information, Oyinlola ti wa si odo mi ri. OYES, won ti wa si odo mi ri; photo won wa nibi. A de ti se orisirisi ise pelu won. Tori e lo je ki a koko bere ise pelu awon eyan nigba ti ilu daa: Kano, Jos,Ibadan,Eko,Abekuta. A ni kaakiri. But nigba ti ilu wa daru, ti ko si nkankan, kaluku tuka. Lafi wa yi si oro contract. Awon eyan o gbiyanju ati ra nkan. Ko si owo. Ounje ni awon eyan ronu si. Nkan ti won de n ko wa lati China, ti government ba le make policy pe nkan ti o ba ti meet standard Nigeria, bi America ti ri, nkan ti o ba ti meet standard won o ni je ki e ko wole

AI: I am not a member of their association but I am in the Manufacturers Association of Nigeria, which I joined 27 years ago. We are currently having some conflict with Government for awarding a contract worth 250 million naira to Aba shoe makers to build 50 thousand pair of shoes, even though they did not have the necessary equipment and capacity to actualize it. We in MAN are curious: Government knows those who have shoe factories, why did they not give us the job? For your information, Oyinlola visited my factory. The OYES team also came and inspected the place. I have photographs to prove it. We have done various projects for them. When the economy was still healthy we had factories in places like Kano, Jos, Ibadan, Lagos and Abeokuta. The economic melt down forced everyone to close shop. So, we resorted to engaging contract staff every time there is work to be done. People do not have power to purchase. They rather spend their earnings on food. Government can enforce the policy that makes it impossible for people to import substandard products from China, like America is doing

WR: e se gan. Nkan ti e n so ni pe this policy pe ki won ma ko nkan wole lati China, pe ki ijoba maa encourage local manufacturers. Sugbon bayi, arin eyin ati awon iyoku yi, bawo lo se ri?

WR: Thank you so much. What you are saying then is that government should check importation from China and instead encourage local manufacturers. Right now, what is the relationship between you and your contemporaries?

AI: mi o tie wa mo enikankan ninu won

AI: I really don't know any of them

WR: awa na o fe ki e mo enikankan. O da bi enipe awon na o mo yin. ikan ninu awon baba yen n so nijo yen pe enikan to je eyan kan soso won fun 5000, awon iyoku ti awon cover gbogbo State, won fun awon ni 10000; owo tie ni yen o je. Ko dabi eni pe o mo yin, boya o gbo ni. mo kan fe beere pe bawon ni arin yin se ri, se ko si?

WR: We hardly expect you to know anyone of them. It seems they don't know you too. The elderly man we mentioned earlier complained that some person got 5000 pairs while they who have members across the state were given 10000, and got more money than they did together. It was not clear whether he knew you; perhaps he was told by someone. I just am curious, what is your relationship with them?

AI: emi o tie da won mo. A o si jo duro papo. Won wa si ile ise mi won si ri pe, awon eleyi ohun ti a fe won o se. won ti e ya foto ile ise wa. Kani Governor raye ni, maa fe ko wa wo ile ise wa but ko le raye

AI: I don't know any of them. We have never stood together to discuss anything before. A delegation was sent to inspect our factory and they were certain that we would deliver if given the job. They took pictures of our factory. If the Governor had been chanced, I am sure he would have suggested he came to see our facility himself but I doubt that he will ever be able to.

WR: e se pupo o

WR: thank you so much

CPSIA information can be obtained
at www.ICGtesting.com
Printed in the USA
LVHW050353110522
718423LV00007B/619

9 783962 032098